EVERYONE IN LA IS AN ASSHOLE

EVERYONE IN LA IS AN ASSHOLE

Everyone In LA Is An Asshole™ *Book One*

SARAH FULLER   SARAH NOFFKE   MICHAEL ANDERLE

L M B P N

DISRUPTIVE IMAGINATION

LMBPN Publishing
PMB 196, 2540 South Maryland Pkwy
Las Vegas, NV 89109

First US edition, November 2018

SARAH'S NOTES

Written October 18, 2018

Writing a book about one's life is no easy feat. I doubted that the events I would tell would be of interests to anyone. I'm used to hiding behind fictional characters and making them do the strange things. All walls had to come down if I was going to make this book worth reading. I knew I couldn't hold back and yet, I didn't want to lose all my friends. In all honesty, I make fun of many in this book, but no one more than myself. It's also important to remember that these accounts are described through my lens. In many cases, the events are told from how I felt about them, rather than how they actually happened.

All names have been changed. Events, people and experiences have been consolidated. I took many liberties with how things happened. Exaggeration was sometimes employed in order to enhance the funny factor. And I maybe made some stuff up.

Sarcasm is used heavily in this book. My ex-husband is an awesome person, hence the reason that I married him.

My family, my friends, and those I interact with are wonderful people. But I make fun of all of them. I didn't want to write a book about how we're all gentle souls who never fuck up. I wanted to talk about the funny stuff we do when we make mistakes, when we try too hard, when we try and navigate our lives.

This book is supposed to be funny and not intended to offend. If it does, then I apologize. I truly love and value all people. I appreciate those in my life. And I hope to make them smile as they read about all the ways I fuck up my life.

Now I can truly say that my life is an open book.

Open her up.

For all four million people in Los Angeles.
You make this city great.
- Sarah

Chapter One

THE BIGGEST ASSHOLE OF THEM ALL

Growing up, I never watched the Beverly Hillbillies and thought, "California is the life for me." However, much like Jed Clampett, I started in the backwoods with enough kinfolk to fill up an acre or two.

Sometimes, if I close my eyes, I can still hear the murky lake beating against the retaining wall. I can see the buoy, bobbing in the waters as the smell of pine and moss wafts through the air. And ten-year-old me is kicking my legs over the deteriorating dock, eyes scanning for water moccasins, the scariest-ass snakes on the planet.

That girl, who grew up in that small town, the one mom said was full of "East Texas Bubbas," never thought she'd live in the City of Angels along with four million other people.

Growing up, we had one stoplight. The nearest store was twenty miles away. We had to cross a bridge to get to said store, which by the way did *not* sell organic produce. It *did* sell cartons of Merit cigarettes, Kool-Aid, bologna and other staples of my childhood home.

In my mind, Los Angeles wasn't a place where people like me lived. It was Mars, a place where Martians lived. And guess what I'm not? I ain't no Martian. Ask my momma. According to her, you could trace our heritage back to the Queen of England, which made no sense to me growing up. I had no college fund and only owned one pair of shoes. Guess we were the forgotten relatives. According to my mother, we stayed after the revolution and gave up our rights to the crown for a better life. I think that made us dumbasses, but she always disagreed as she clipped coupons for cigarettes.

Unlike Jed Clampett, I didn't strike black gold on the fifteen acres that bordered our house. I didn't buy a mansion in Beverly Hills next to a banker. I live in a town-house a stone's throw from Malibu (if a giant was throwing the stone). My neighbor is a history teacher who gives me cookies from Costco because I'm too cheap to get my own membership.

In contrast to Jed Clampett, I ended up in LA quite by accident. If I could go back and tell my ten-year-old self anything (besides to invent Facebook), it would be that Los Angeles *is* Mars and totally awesome. It's the strangest place I've ever seen, with its movie stars and divas. The vegans clog the store aisles, discussing arrowroot and potato starch. The power executives smoke with their windows down as they sit in the parking lot known as the 101 freeway. They aren't fooling anyone with their cigarettes hanging outside the window of their Audi. They are totally getting dinged for smoking in *that* lease.

And then there's me: a divorced science fiction writer with a child and a cat and a true devotion to the place I call home.

I might have thought that LA was full of Martians, but what I didn't realize is that one day, I'd revel in the fact that I am one. Like a lot of people in this vast city, I'm opinionated, liberal, eccentric and let's be honest, a real asshole. Guess what? I drink bottled water. It's true. And for the life of me, I can't fucking park my Prius. It's always hanging over the white line. I sincerely mean to repark the car, but then I don't want to be late to Pilates class.

I might call the people in LA assholes, but it's out of love. Taking ourselves too seriously is never advised. LA is unlike any place on Earth; that's why I make fun of it and its citizens.

There are some very strange things that happen here. Things that only the locals know.

Dating in this city is about like trying to find your soulmate at the zoo. There's a lot of options, none of which are acceptable unless you want fleas or to be mauled. However, you keep holding out hope that the monkeys will evolve, or your standards will dip so low that the sloth starts looking more appealing.

I have a friend who has told me the easiest way to find Mr. Right is to relocate out of LA. She contends that the market here is too competitive. Possibly she's right, and there are too many options in this city. It's easy to swipe left when there are a million other chimps ready to disappoint me in their unique fashion. And why should the men settle on me when there are hippos all over this city who are just as appealing with their long eyelashes and chunky thighs? I'm not calling anyone fat. I'm following this analogy until the bitter end.

No one in this city wants to settle. We have too many options. If a guy isn't trending, then how do I know if he is a good life partner?

My problem though is a bit more complex. I'm not just a thirty-something-year-old trying to date in this city full of shabby-chic-shiny dipshits. I'm one of those, yes, but I'm also...a science fiction author.

I know you'd think that, as a science fiction writer, I'd have guys lining up to put a ring on this. Although, to be honest, I loathe rings. Furthermore, the institution of marriage lost its favor with me when I flunked out of it after my tenth year. The first time the state of California made me pay dearly for not wanting to be in a bad relationship anymore, I sort of lost those romantic feelings toward marriage. I still have nightmares about the divorce paperwork.

But I digress.

My friends tell me that when a guy reads "sci-fi writer" in my dating profile, he immediately thinks of X-Files. I'm no Scully if we're being honest.

My friend Cheryl (her name wasn't changed to protect her because I'm an asshole) says that she reads my books and doesn't consider them sci-fi, which I think makes me a bad sci-fi writer. She said I write sci-fi for those who don't normally like the genre. *Say what?* In other words, I make the Frappuccino of sci-fi novels. If you hate coffee, no worries. The sugar and whipped cream masks the coffee bean flavor. I apparently douse my books with syrup and sprinkles.

Cheryl says that when guys read "sci-fi" in my dating profile, they think of Outer Limits and automatically assume I wear a tinfoil hat while sitting in my storm shelter, playing Dungeons and Dragons.

That's the furthest thing from the truth. I don't have a storm shelter. I live in California, not the horrible state of Texas, where I was born and raised. Don't judge.

"Just put that you're a romance writer," Cheryl encouraged. "Everyone likes them."

I don't think so, asshole-friend. The only seductive bare chests on my book covers belong to aliens with three heads and tentacles.

My publisher counseled me on my dating life, because once again I'm too cheap to shell out for therapy. Taking pity on my plight, he suggested I go to Comic-Con to find a guy who shared my similar interests. Because I'm an idiot as well as an asshole, I replied, "There are no attractive men at Comic-Con." Then realizing my blunder, I added, "Not you! Not you! I meant to say, there are no attractive, *single* men at Comic-Con!"

To be honest, there are probably tons of passable, potential mates at Comic-Con who have good faces. My problem is finding them. Part of my dilemma might be that I prefer to hang out with the characters in my head on a Saturday night. They don't talk back, but they also don't shut up when I tell them to. *Yes,* I've just admitted to talking to the voices in my head. Apparently, another thing my friends say I shouldn't announce on my dating profile.

There are so many pretentious rules with dating: Clean under your nails, shave, don't make more than three Doctor Who references at dinner.

My Pilates instructor has no problem getting a date, but she also regularly talks to people who are *real.* My other single friends fumble regularly but tell me the key is to get out there. I've taken off my tinfoil hat and decided that they might be right.

I'm nervous. I'm reluctant. I have sky-high expectations. Let's be honest, I'm judgmental and quick to call innocent people names. And I'm certainly annoyed by the pretenses that wrap LA up into a ball of hair extensions. However, I also realize I'm not so innocent. I'm no Elly May Clampett, as much as I wish I were. I may be from the backwoods, but I was born for this city. In truth, I might tease my fellow LA peeps, but I'm the biggest asshole of them all.

Chapter Two

HOOKER SHOES AND OTHER NAMES I CALL MY EX-HUSBAND'S GIRLFRIENDS

Because the universe loves irony, my divorce was finalized a couple of days before our eleventh wedding anniversary. My soon-to-be ex-husband called me the day before things were official and asked if I wanted to go to a celebratory dinner—his treat! That sounded a bit like having a party at a funeral, but I love free food and, more importantly, free wine.

I accepted, and we went to dinner. In hindsight, I should have ordered the steak. Scratch that. I should have ordered *two* steaks. One for dinner and one to take home. Instead, I got the burrito, an entrée I only order when I don't care how I look as I cram a giant steak-filled tortilla into my mouth.

Although my ex-husband, George, apparently wanted the dinner to just be the two of us, I wasn't booking a babysitter for such an occasion. Therefore, our daughter sat between us at a Mexican restaurant, painting her face with refried beans as George gave me tentative stares across the table. I was pretty certain he was having second thoughts about this whole "divorce" business, which was absolutely non-negotiable for me.

We made small talk, mostly about my career as a sci-fi writer. As usual, he voiced his concerns about whether it would pan out. I tried to pretend I had big plans for my books.

Honestly, I was days away from charging into the closest university and telling them why they needed me. "I'm a great professor! I know about accreditation. I can calculate student learning outcomes and, although I find the work soul-sucking, I will do it with a smile." No one, up until this moment, knows that I was close to caving, putting my writing life on hold to take a job that would support my little one and me.

In the parking lot of the restaurant, George said a fond farewell, like he was never going to see me again, hugging me with a bit too much closeness. I shook my head, thinking that he was going home to a freezer full of Ben and Jerry's, which he'd consume while playing the musical *Rent* on loop.

That night, I received a call from George.

Here it is, I thought.

I just knew he was lying in his empty bathtub with a bottle of bourbon, burning old pictures of us. The least I could do was accept his phone call, although the Sims was calling my name.

"Hello," I said, my voice hesitant like I was answering a suicide hotline.

"Hey, I need to talk to you."

Of course, he does. I paused my game and took a seat in my armchair, the one I reserved for long conversations.

"I was hoping that tonight it would have just been the two of us, without Eleanor," George said.

Of course, he was.

"There's something I need to tell you," George continued, ushered on by my silence. "It's the reason I asked you to dinner."

My stomach rumbled, probably because I needed more steak. "I thought you wanted to cheers to our divorce."

"I did, but there was something else I wanted to clink glasses to," George answered.

I thought hard. It was close to Mother's Day. Over a decade earlier, I really should have chosen a wedding date better, but the venue was discounted that weekend. Years later, I'd realize why. When I was just about to thank him for acknowledging the things I'd happily sacrificed to be a mother and commend him on cherishing that, he said, "Sarah, I'm dating someone, *and* she's amazing."

Silence.

I looked around, wondering why I wasn't drinking. Then my mind searched desperately for the exact reason *this* was wrong. It hit me like a bullet.

"Are you fucking telling me that you took me out the day before our divorce to celebrate the fact that you're in a relationship?" I won't lie. I yelled. Thankfully, my daughter was at George's house, where she was probably cold and poorly tucked into her slanted bed covered in dirty sheets.

"Well...I...It's just—"

"Did you just describe this person as 'amazing,' like that

was at all necessary in this initial description?" I continued, cutting George off.

"She *is* amazing, and if you just gave her a chance—"

"Whoa!" I yelled, clear and loud. "She's not moving in, is she? We need rules. Boundaries. Eleanor can't have women paraded in and out of her life." I took a breath.

What he needed was fucking class, but I reminded myself that George was my ex-husband for a reason. He had taken me out the day before our divorce not to celebrate, but to gloat. Real-fucking-classy.

"Seriously, Sarah, if you just give her a chance—"

"Look, Hooker Shoes and I aren't in a relationship," I said, instantly coining a name that would follow this woman around for the next twelve months. "Eleanor needs her parents and not to be confused. Let's give her time to adjust. Then we introduce slutty girlfriends. Cool?"

I might have been a bit harsh. The wine and steak swam to my head right then. George started in on why his new girlfriend was so "amazing," and all I could think about was how he'd invited me on a "celebration," looking all remorse-ful...or so I'd thought. I'd mistaken his tentative expression for nervousness. He'd been trying to tell me about Hooker Shoes the whole night, because the right time to do that was obviously on the eve of our divorce.

I'm not going to lie. I hung up on him.

The next morning, I awoke to the sound of two competing noises. The first was my phone, ringing with a number I recognized, but hadn't expected—a publisher. The other noise was an incessant knocking at my door. I picked up the phone and cleared my throat.

"Hello," I said, trying to not sound like I'd been asleep

seconds prior.

"Hello, Sarah," the voice on the other end said.

It was an up-and-coming publisher. One that I wanted to work with for more than a few reasons.

I tried to listen to the opportunity unfolding on the other side of the line as I hopped around my bedroom, trying to dress. The knocking continued downstairs. Either someone wanted to sell me magazines subscriptions badly, or my neighbor was mad that I'd parked over the line yet again. *Seriously, people, I need to go back to Driver's Ed. It's not my fucking fault that I learned how to drive in a one-horse town. We parked in open pastures. There were no fucking lines!*

"Yes, I've heard of the new universes you're creating," I said, hustling downstairs, moments away from pulling out a butcher knife before answering the door. Whoever was knocking didn't understand that, after two minutes, *move on to the next house, buddy. I don't want your magazine subscriptions.*

I listened to the publisher, anxious to hear about the new opportunity as I looked through the peephole.

Then my heart sank.

George stood on the other side of my door, his fist continuing to pound. So he had no clue *and* no manners. Single moms sleep in on the Tuesdays they don't have their children. Everyone knows that. It was his day to get her to school, not mine.

I opened the door and waved him in, giving him a threatening look as I pointed him to the chair in the corner, or as I like to call it, "Time-fucking-out."

"Anyway, if you're interested in coming on board," the voice on the other end of the line continued, "we'd be happy to have you."

Happy? This was the break I'd been looking for without knowing it. I'd always thought that I'd publish solo. When that hadn't worked and George had told me I'd better get a "real" job, I'd pretty much unfolded my ancient resume and decided that my kid would go into daycare while I worked in an office. But this... *this* was my chance. It was something new.

Later, I'd appreciate how my *new* life was ringing on the phone while my *old* life was knocking at the door.

George had banged incessantly on my door to get my attention on the official day of our divorce because I'd acted uncharacteristically. I'd hung up and refused to talk to him. But in my defense, it was the first time he'd asked me to a celebratory dinner to cheers to his new girlfriend, Hooker Shoes.

Fun fact: Everyone, from my dental hygienist to my stylist, still calls this poor woman "Hooker Shoes." I can't help it that I'm amazing at naming "amazing" people.

Although George didn't appreciate my colorful name, he was reasonable enough to agree that we both wouldn't introduce anyone to Eleanor until they'd been in our life for a year. Fine by me, since I wasn't planning on introducing her to anyone for a long time. I wanted to look like the good parent, not the one ready to put my smokies back in the campfire so soon after the forest burned down.

Over the next year, the world around us got used to our divorce. I didn't make a Facebook announcement about our status change. I just let it organically come out as I spoke to people. And, man, do I wish I would have made a Facebook announcement so that all the assholes could have gotten used to it in one fell swoop.

I get that a divorce affects more than the ones it happens to, but I had more people apologize to me that year than when my brother died. Here's why that's wrong: George and I didn't give up, we grew apart. We tried. It didn't work. We were all suffering, including Eleanor. Being apart was better for everyone.

Don't feel sorry for me for quitting something that didn't work. That's like showing remorse to someone for quitting a bad habit. *'Oh, Jim, I heard you gave up drinking. I'm sorry.'*

Drinking was going to kill Jim! Don't apologize! I get that my relationship was probably not going to directly kill me, but we were going to demoralize each other enough that heart disease was going to strike hard and fast.

I had someone contact me and say, "I'm not going to lie, your divorce was a real kick in the stomach."

I gulped as I counted backward from ten. What I wanted to say couldn't come out, which was, "Oh man, sorry my life change was so hard on you. I'll consider that the next time I make a choice for my family's happiness."

The honest truth is we have to allow people to quit. Whether it's a job, people, substances, habits. It challenges us when the people around us change. Them not being the same is hard, but does it have to be? I'm not entirely the same as I was before the divorce. I daresay I'm better. Happier. Free. But I challenged those who knew me before, and for that, I'm not sorry.

I'm not entirely sure how long Hooker Shoes stuck around. She was there long enough to give my daughter a few gifts, though. The first was a curling iron. Do you know what a five-year-old doesn't need? If you guessed candy, alcohol, or hot irons, then you're correct. My child's baby-thin hair didn't need to be seared at three hundred and eighty degrees.

But guess what happens when you share fifty-fifty custody: Sometimes you have to shut the fuck up and like it. So I didn't say anything about Hooker Shoes leaving her stuff around for Eleanor to play with, even though these objects created second-degree burns. That's how I'm the bigger person.

However, one day my fifteen-year-old sister called me. Yes, I have a sister who is twenty years younger than me. It's how we keep things interesting.

"Hey, Weirdo," Trix said on the other side of the line.

"What do you want?" I answered.

"So, Hooker Shoes just sent me a friend request on Instagram."

I laughed. "Oh man, what a creep. Why would she do that?"

"Probably saw that I was connected with George and wanted to build bridges," Trix answered.

I thought of the blasted bridge I had to cross every morning on the way to school in the backwoods of Texas. I always thought I'd die trying to get across that thing, like it would sink into the lake.

"Wonder what she said when you rejected her request,"

I mused.

Silence.

"Trix?" I questioned, sensing the tension.

"I didn't want to make Brother George mad," she said, using her nickname for him. "I accepted, and then Hooker Shoes liked all my photos."

"Because that's not strange," I said.

So now I had this crazy, obsessed person who I was afraid of getting close to my daughter going after my sister. Shit was getting real.

"Unfriend her," I ordered.

"But—"

Big sisters call the shots. Always. "Do it now, Trix."

She agreed, worried she was going to cause a wedge between George and Hooker Shoes.

"Not a problem," I assured Trix.

I planned on buying the biggest wedge heels to kick this woman with if she didn't back off my family. End of story. Trix was *my* sister, not George's, and this stranger was trespassing on *my* territory. *Back-the-fuck-up*.

I told George, "How would you feel if my boyfriend sent your sister a friend request and stalked her on social media?"

He agreed that it would be kind of strange. However, *my* sister is a minor, so it was a bit creepier than if my imaginary boyfriend was friendly with his sister.

I thought I was done with Hooker Shoes for a while. I even thought that the two had broken up, which, I'll be honest, would be for the best. I told George, "You introduced her all wrong. Try with a new girl and, this time, don't mention that she's 'amazing' and don't take me to dinner to tell me about her. Say she is a person and the best you can do, and we'll move on. Meanwhile, I'll know that you still cry yourself to sleep because I'm not yours." That was the healthy approach, here.

Shortly after Christmas, a year after George met Hooker Shoes, my blood pressure began to rise steadily. Every day, I waited for him to call to arrange "the meeting." The one where sweet, innocent Eleanor would have to meet a woman in shoes like stilts.

George had told Eleanor about his girlfriend finally, which she thought was hilarious. Me, not so much.

"She should know I'm in a relationship," he argued.

"Because she's Sally Jesse Raphael!"

I get that my references aren't timely, but I still didn't understand why our five-year-old needed to be learning all the details of her father's romantic relationship.

That's why I held a firm front. "Honey, I don't have a boyfriend, because you're all I need," I told Eleanor. Two can play at that game.

Christmas came and went, and the time when George had all but promised "the meeting" passed. One day, Eleanor had an event at her school: "Bring A Stuffed Animal" day. I picked her up that afternoon to see her carrying a giant wolf stuffed animal she'd brought from her father's house.

"Hey, baby," I said, eyeing the rabid-looking wolf with unease. "That's the animal you chose to bring?"

She nodded. "Daddy told me to bring it. His girlfriend gave it to me for Christmas."

I halted. "Wait. Hoo—" I caught myself. "You met that woman?"

Eleanor shook her head. "No, but she sent it to me as a present."

I nodded like that made sense, like sending gifts to children you haven't met but want to like you is cool. I mean, what I knew of this woman so far was that she preyed on minors like my sister, so of course, I had low expectations. Oh, and I knew she was "amazing," according to George.

"Isn't the wolf cool?" Eleanor asked from the backseat.

"It's big," I said, noticing how it took up two seats. "And isn't it nice that your father asked you to bring it to *my* house? How thoughtful. When we get home, leave it in the car so we can find the right place for it to *live*."

Eleanor agreed. She went inside when we got home and did what children do best with worthless gifts: she forgot about it. When she was sleeping in her cozy bed, all tucked in perfectly, her sheets cleaned and pressed, I went to my car and got the stuffed animal. I then chucked it into the trash, where it belonged.

To my relief, things apparently dissolved between Hooker Shoes and George, making it so I didn't have to worry about this strange woman entering Eleanor's life. It's not that I'm opposed to her specifically. It's really that everything started off wrong with that one.

Since then, George and I have spoken about how better to handle things. Our initial wounds after the divorce have healed. And I've asked for his girlfriends to not stalk my sister, which I find an easy request.

Later, when George asked where the giant stuffed animal had gone, I truthfully said, "I don't know." It was an honest answer because I seriously don't know where the trash goes when it leaves my house.

Chapter Three

NO ONE IN LA HAS THEIR OWN HAIR

When I was six months pregnant with Eleanor, George's company was moved to Los Angeles. At the time, we were living in the quiet Rogue Valley in Southern Oregon. The area spent half the year in fog and the other half alternating between fresh showers and cheery sunlight. I'd heard about the Californians. They sold their small bungalows in San Fran or So-Cal and moved up to unsoiled Oregon with buckets of money, buying the mansions on the top of the mountains so they could look down on the rest of us.

I was adamant that we couldn't move to LA and raise our child there. I just knew that she'd be handed an inhaler upon entering the city and have to choose which gang to align with. Most of my views on LA were formed in the 1990's from snippets on the news of gang fights in the streets. Compton was the central hub of the city, right? You couldn't get through there without showing your gang signs —get them wrong, and you were going down.

However, I also knew that if we stayed in Oregon, I'd

have to be the main breadwinner and, although I didn't mind that, I really wanted to be the main caregiver. You see, I'm never happy.

George and I moved to Oregon shortly after getting married because I thought I was a hippie. I got rid of my car and joined a co-op. I took jobs working for eccentrics who didn't value the fact that I had a Master's in business and were more concerned with what my astrological sign was. I was seriously hired as the assistant to a government contractor because I'm a Virgo. I ended up quitting that job after six months because it turns out I'm not a hippie, I'm a fucking yuppie.

What can I say, I like wearing shoes and washing my hair.

Reluctantly, I took a trip to explore LA when I was uber pregnant. The six-lane highways were a drastic change from the streets in Oregon, which were quiet and lined with planters overflowing with dangling flowers. The beach was minutes away instead of a three-hour trek along the Oregon trail, during which I always felt sick with a unique form of dysentery, brought on by George's bad driving. And the biggest surprise was there were options. The city stretched out like a lotus flower upon my arrival, a thousand petals bursting with unique neighborhoods.

Sure, there was crime. There were places where we kept the car moving, pretending that the buildings covered in graffiti were art exhibits. But most importantly, there was something that we didn't have in Oregon. Something that had worried me from the moment I realized I was having a little human. Oregon, a mostly rural state, has about as much diversity as a kangaroo ranch in the outback.

Although it was clean and safe, I worried that my child would have the same sheltered upbringing that I did. But in *LA*, there was diversity. A melting pot—which meant a wide variety of cuisines.

Let's be honest, this was always going to be about the food.

Oregon had boutique wineries and artisan cheeses, which are the cornerstone of my existence. However, there is a frozen yogurt shop on every corner in LA, usually bordered by restaurants that have several hundred yelp reviews. I'd gone to the same three restaurants in Oregon for years. The choices in LA overwhelmed me in all the right ways.

I will forever think fondly of Oregon, where the *real* people are modest, the hippies are weird and the new age gurus are subtly annoying. I had one metaphysical boss tell me that I wasn't being my authentic self. The movie *I Heart Huckabees* puts it best: "How am I not myself?"

I then ate those words when I came to LA and learned exactly what he meant. He was wrong because he was a dirty metaphysical teacher who spoke about souls like he was God himself, but still, I later came to understand fake. And you know what, I didn't hate it. I found it entertaining. Funny. A part of a culture that churns out the entertainment the rest of the world relishes.

As a teenager, I watched *Clueless* approximately thirty-one and a half times. I wanted to be Alicia Silverstone's character, Cher. I wanted my best friend to be like Dionne, although she wasn't black. There was only one black person in all of East Texas, and he was banned from playing football for no apparent reason. Because what's the worst thing you can do to someone in East Texas? Not allow them to play the holy game of football.

Even back in 1995, I found Cher's fakery entertaining. What I didn't find cool was the fact that she kissed her stepbrother. I don't care how you spin that one, it's just wrong.

Beverly Hills and the surrounding areas of Los Angeles have come a long way since *Clueless* came out. So much so, that it makes the movie look like Little House on the Prairie in LA.

I've been in this city for several years, and still the outgoing personalities and antics of the locals are never lost on me. I moved away for a little while and was reminded of its absurdities soon after I returned. My mom friends hosted a brunch to welcome me back to LA, while our kids were hard at work at school.

My flexible schedule as a writer allows me to brunch on a Wednesday, or really any day. Well, that is until I realize that I've put off a book too long and have two days to write thirty-five thousand words to meet the deadline. It's then that I wish I was into speed or Adderall.

Apparently, it's sort of a wonder that I've been able to write as many books as I have without being an Adderall junkie. Imagine my surprise when I learned that high-powered executives were harassing ADHD children on the playground for their Adderall. Long gone are the days of bullying kids for their lunch money. No way. Now the CEOs want little Timmy's prescription drugs. This is why I can't do corporate America.

Back to brunch. At the table, my friend filled my glass with champagne while I explained how much I'd missed the city. I protested her large pour, explaining that I couldn't show up to pick up my kid from school sauced. That's when the woman beside me clicked her tongue. "You're back in LA now. Everyone is on something, always."

The point was reinforced on another day when I went to the doctor to get Botox. Yes, I've gotten Botox, but more for medical reasons than superficial ones. I look at the computer so much that my right eyebrow twitches if I don't subdue it with drugs. I have to tranquilize that bitch or I can't get any work done.

Anyway, the doctor is about to stick me with Botox, and he pauses.

"Have you been drinking?" he asked me.

I sniffed the hoodie that I might not have washed in a day or two. "No, it's ten in the morning."

He laughed. "It doesn't matter what time it is. In my Beverly Hills' office, my actresses are toasted on mimosas by this time."

How charming, I thought. I wished I had a job where I could be sauced by mid-morning. Then I remembered that I *did*, but I also couldn't be so drunk that I'd fall off the reformer machine during my noon Pilates class. Everyone loves a drunk until she makes a scene in class. Then you become *that* person.

So I'm at brunch with my friends, casually sipping my champagne, when the same woman who informed me that everyone in LA is drunk or high reaches over and pulls on my hair. Since I wasn't on the playground, and this wasn't second grade, I turned to her, wondering what strange LA behavior this was. I'd spent a year and a half in central California where the people do things "differently," meaning they are sort of normal. It's totally boring.

"Is this real?" the woman asked me, continuing to pull on my hair.

I yanked my hair out of her hands, wondering if she meant the wool sweater I was wearing and was just too drunk to figure out the difference.

"My sweater?" I asked.

She'd told me that she shouldn't be drinking since she didn't have a gallbladder anymore, but that didn't stop her. It wouldn't have stopped me, either.

"No, I meant your hair," she said, again reaching over to tug on a strand.

I was thoroughly entertained by this, but feigned offense. "Of course it is. Why wouldn't it be?"

She then pulled a mane of hair free from her head, holding it high in the air over the scrambled eggs on the brunch table. "Because mine isn't. Come on, no one in LA has their own hair."

I've since learned that she's mostly right. For a while, I thought every woman was popping prenatal vitamins to get their thick tresses. A trip to a wine bar in Solvang was quite illuminating. Solvang is this cute little Danish town north of LA that the yuppies congest on the weekends with their Land Rovers and picnic baskets from Bed Bath and Beyond.

I told the girl next to me at the wine bar that she had nice hair. "I'd have to sacrifice a goat to get hair like that."

She giggled. "I would too." She then pulled the curtain of hair aside to show me a row of seams where her real hair met the fake stuff. It then turned into a show-and-tell moment, as six other women joined in, showing off their hair extensions.

I think LA is cool. I love the people. I get Botox to tranquilize my overworked eyebrows. However, I'm way too low maintenance for hair extensions. But don't think I haven't thought about it. I *do* take prenatals, biotin, and collagen, all in an attempt to add a couple of inches to my hair. When it comes to attaching something to my body, though, I draw the line. I've always been a tomboy, which is just my way of saying that I have zero fashion sense and I'm too lazy to comb my hair.

There's a place across the parking lot from my Pilates studio that advertises itself as a "bar." I was all excited when it moved into the shopping center, thinking of the convenience factor. I can't drink before Pilates, but there's no reason I can't grab a cocktail afterward. I have a whole two hours before I have to pick up Eleanor.

However, my instructor popped my bubble one day when I told her I was heading to this new bar across the way. That's when she informed me that the Blink Bar was a place where ladies go to get fake eyelashes "installed." I'd like to put a stop to calling things bars that don't exclusively serve alcohol. That's just wrong. That's like calling strip clubs "The Office." Deceptively, you can't get a drink at this Blink Bar. And how could I even drink while someone is gluing fake eyelashes to my face? There is smart multitasking, but that is not it.

Growing up in Texas, the old church ladies would smile at me and say, "Oh, bless your heart," which simply meant, "You're a dumbass." In Oregon, the people are polite enough to never tell you what they are thinking. However, in LA, the place where everyone is considered fake, I have found people to be the most real. They might have foreheads so smooth you could ice skate on them, more hair that is fake than real, and extremely distracting, long eyelashes—seriously, that's all I can focus on when looking at someone with extensions—but they are real in their hearts. At least, the ones I've met.

Chapter Four

I SHOWER REGULARLY

I'm thirty-seven years old and have an online dating profile, so shit is obviously going according to plan.

Apparently, people don't meet each other at the coffee shops or pharmacies anymore. Gone are the days of bumping into a guy in a parking lot and having him ask for my number. If I do bump into someone, it's because I'm on my damn phone, swiping through potential matches on a dating app.

My friends Robert and Colleen met in a parking lot over twenty years ago. She was trying to get into his car because it looked exactly like hers. When he told her that, she was adamant that he was wrong. He then pointed two rows over to where an almost identical car sat but that one brandished a scratch over the right fender . He asked for Colleen's number, and they've been living the hippie life in Oregon ever since. However, these days, if I see a guy trying to get into my car, I'm calling the police on his ass. This makes me wonder if, unbeknown to me, I've sent Mr. Right to jail. I have called the police on a few suspicious characters over the years.

Dating apps are how singles meet these days. There's Tinder for the hookups. Apparently, it has the most options, with over 100 million users. Isn't it strange that there are so many single people out there looking for love, and yet there's so much loneliness in the world? Sorry, had an introspective moment there. I promise not to do it again.

Coffee Meets Bagel is an app for those looking for a long-term relationship. I like the idea of qualifiers because, let's be honest, I'm fucking picky. This app, like most, has a time constraint. After a week, your conversations with a match disappear. It's an attempt to force matches to meet up and not draw things out with long text messaging. In other words, don't waste my time with sweet poetry. Let's meet. If we click, great. If not, move on.

I like this approach. I've respected the guys who after only a few messages ask me out on a date. It's better than the guy who sent me long paragraphs for weeks amounting to a relationship that fizzled out because I got carpal tunnel trying to respond to all his talking points. And it's way better than the guy who tries to pretend he's someone else in chat. How do they not know they'll be caught?

I had this one guy tell me that he loved to read. I asked him, "What are some of your favorite authors?"

Because everyone in LA is an asshole and has to be a douche, he says, "Mostly Hemingway."

And because I'm an asshole, I countered with, "Name one. Just name one Hemingway novel."

Complete silence.

The dude couldn't throw out a single Hemingway title. Twenty-two options, and the guy had nothing because he was a poser who had never read a single book by Hemingway. I'm not pretending that I spend my evenings by the fire reading *For Whom the Bell Tolls*, but I also don't throw out pretentious shit.

Maybe that's my problem. When asked what authors I read, I'm too quick to say "Phillip Pullman, JK Rowling, and F. Scott Fitzgerald." And yes, I actually read Fitzgerald. I have almost every line of *The Great Gatsby* memorized. I keep hoping to meet a guy like Jay Gatsby on one of these dating apps, but I think he is being lame, standing on a pier and pining after some slut.

The dating app that I choose to waste time on is Bumble. I made the conscientious decision to go with this app because I have zero game. The other day, a super attractive guy at my gym ran after me in the parking lot. I thought he was going to tell me that I had my skirt tucked into my underwear...yet again. Instead, he sidled up next to me and said, "Hey, wasn't that class hard?"

Since then, I've learned he was trying to make a move. Did I agree that the full body workout we'd just done together was strenuous? Did I try and bond with him over how mean the instructor was? Oh no. Instead, I treated him like he was a beggar on the streets of Santa Monica and acted like I was a French tourist that didn't speak proper English.

I nodded. Backed away. Kept my head down and said, "*Oui, oui. Au revoir.*" I then hustled to my car, wondering why the fuck I was speaking French.

Shockingly, the guy has never tried to speak to me again.

It is because of my horrible game with guys that I chose Bumble. It's the app where the girl must make the first move. I'm trying to push myself out of my comfort zone.

After I match with a guy, I usually comb through his profile and pick out the things I relate to. Then I offer him way too much information about myself and blow the whole thing. This has happened so often that my girlfriends have intervened.

"Just say 'hey' and offer a single compliment," Alissa, a fellow single gal, advised.

To be honest, many of the guys don't give a lot to go off on. I've encountered more than one profile where the guy has bragged about "showering regularly." When did that even become part of a bio? Shouldn't it be a given?

I find myself looking past many things when reviewing profiles. My standards have sunk. At first, I was strict, swiping left over a thousand times for every swipe right. Then the same guys got rotated back into the lineup, and I realized that I'd gone through every guy in LA on Bumble.

I don't feel that my expectations are too far off. I want a guy who isn't too tall or too short. Medium. No hipsters; I would only bring them down. However, I fear my expectations will have to shift even further. When did everyone in LA become a fucking lumberjack with a full beard and wearing flannel? Damn hipsters! This is the newest trend in LA, making most of the twenty-something guys look like they're in their forties with these giant beards. Can we start a razor drive for these guys?

Hear ye! Hear ye! Free shaves if you take off your red flannel shirt and donate it to a Canadian!

Sometimes it's difficult to tell the homeless from the

eccentric, wealthy hipsters. I'm afraid to strike up a conversation with one of them only to get mugged.

Most on Bumble in LA are too cool for school. Everyone has a profile pic of them at Machu Picchu. I'm not kidding. I related this to Alissa, and she said, "Why do you think I made a point to go there last year?"

I was stunned. "You hiked up a mountain for four days to get a dating profile pic of you at Machu Picchu?"

"Yeah, and since then, I've made a ton more matches," she stated victoriously. She then related that one guy saw that photo of her and wasn't mesmerized by the ancient temples behind her, but was rather unimpressed by her giant behind.

"Sarah, he literally messaged me and said, 'I didn't realize you were so fat when we first matched.'"

I wanted to be shocked, but Bumble has desensitized me. I matched with a guy who sent me roughly a dozen full body shots of himself standing around in various places. I thought it was weird but commended him on his ability to stand around.

"Did you go to college for that?" I joked.

He didn't think that was funny. The guy was on a mission. "I'm only wondering why you *don't* have any full body shots in *your* profile."

I dropped my slice of pizza and gawked at the phone. *Is he fucking calling me fat?*

I responded with, "I just don't have a camera person following me around. All I have are selfies."

Was that true? Probably not. But damn, men in LA are shallow. I deleted that guy and then went on the Keto diet the next day. I fucking miss pizza!

I realize that it's not just men who are shallow. I swipe left on tattoos, beards, redheads, giants, and men who play hockey.

My friend who is a dental hygienist told me that she had a guy she could set me up with. "He's smart, good-looking and really successful."

"Cool, let's do it," I said, lying in the dentist's chair—one of my favorite places on Earth, because I'm weird like that.

"There's only one thing."

Of course, there is.

"He still has a few baby teeth," she stated.

"Are you fucking kidding me?" I asked. "How old is he?"

"Mid-thirties," she answered. "It's not his fault. He just never lost them, but seriously, he's nice."

"I can't date Baby Teeth," I said. "The offer is off."

I thought she was going to poke me in the gums with one of her sharp instruments. Instead, she nodded, her eyes understanding, framed by her face mask. "I get it. I once wouldn't date a guy because he was a waiter."

I gawked at my friend. "Fuck, you're shallow. A guy could get a new job, but Baby Teeth is on the tooth fairy's shit-list forever. He held out on her."

My dental hygienist laughed. "Well, it was less about his job as a waiter and more about him being clueless. He showed up here right before his shift at the Cheesecake Factory. I went to meet him, and he held out his arms, wearing this long apron. He said, 'I decided to ask you out right before work because I know a woman can't resist a man in uniform.'"

I laughed, making her have to pull the instruments out of my mouth.

"Damn, well, good thing you dodged that bullet. What a clueless moron. Although free cheesecake would have been nice."

She sighed. "I guess, but the man I married is an idiot, too."

"Oh, did you meet him on a dating app?"

She shook her head, leaning down low. "No, I met him in *this* office. He's the dentist."

Chapter Five

I SHOULD ONLY DATE PILOTS

After one week swiping on Bumble, I had carpal tunnel and three dates set up. One with an Italian, one with a Brazilian and the last with a Russian. Unsurprisingly, they were all in the entertainment industry.

Over the week, I texted with these guys, all of them on their best behavior. After over a decade with a nice, Midwestern boy, I felt like I was having an international buffet of men. What made it better was that two of them had accents; however, they also didn't have class, and both canceled our first date.

I don't live in NoHo or the Valley, like all the cool kids in LA. I live on the other side of Malibu where the schools are fantastic, and the coyotes still own the streets. Although I'm only twenty miles away from Hollywood, I might as well live on the other side of the fucking world. When the Russian and the Brazilian learned how far away I was, they both backed out of the date, probably picturing sitting in traffic for eons over the course of our relationship.

The Italian, though, he had class. We figured out a halfway point and planned a date.

It's now that I must make a confession. You know how some creepy men only prey on disadvantaged women? I have that same problem, but it's with redheads. I totally don't get where it came from and, like an addict, I've been trying to stop ever since I realized the flaw in my personality.

It all started with a character who I wrote into my first book, a middle-aged man who was a British redhead with a bad attitude. I was totally obsessed with this character, and so were the readers. He was powerful, brilliant and a complete asshole. He was, in essence, my alter ego. The character then went on to appear in two series. And because I couldn't get enough of his snark, he got his own five-book series.

Now, mind you, I'd never even been around gingers. My oldest sister is one, but if you think we've spent much time together, you're wrong. She's ten years older than me and a pagan who lives off the grid and runs Renaissance fairs. I have zero interest in eating a turkey leg and having my aura read by a gypsy, so Dee and I don't catch up...ever. Oh, and she also doesn't have a phone since she literally lives in the middle of nowhere.

Anyway, somewhere along the line, I developed this disorder where I attract redheads. Notice how I put that: *I attract them.* I'm like a dark place that's accepting of their soullessness, drawing them to me. Before this Bumble business, I had dated three redheads back-to-back-to-back. *I know!* You're wondering how I'd even found *that* many. They come to me. It's weird.

After the last one, I swore off redheads forever... or so I thought. Shawn was a young engineer who seemed nice, however, on our first date, he described himself as a Slytherin. That's like saying, "I'm a bad person." Did I ditch him and go and find a good Gryffindor boy? Did I politely excuse myself from the date, knowing you never piss off a redhead? No, I tried to change him, arguing that he should retake the Sorting Hat quiz.

Turns out he's totally a Slytherin.

"Oh, Sarah," my friend Zoe said, consoling me after I told her about Shawn. "That's a red flag. You run from a Slytherin. There's no changing them."

"I don't really appreciate your use of the word 'red' in this instance," I told her.

She shrugged. "What if I set you up with someone? Are you okay with Jews?"

I thought for a moment. "Why wouldn't I be? Aren't they the ones who wouldn't have me, since I'm all...you know, not Jewish?"

She nodded. "Sometimes people don't want to mix because of the religious aspect."

I was more concerned with the fact that they might be overly hairy, but I didn't say anything about that. "Yeah, call your matchmaker and get me a date with a nice Jewish man."

I'm still waiting on that call.

So back to my first Bumble date. The Italian and I decided to meet at a dark restaurant bar on a Sunday night. Upon meeting, I was pleasantly surprised. He wasn't too short or too tall. He had a nice smile, and the conversation was easy from the start. Everything was going great until he said, "...yeah, well, and because I'm a redhead—"

I slammed my wine glass down and leaned across the table, squinting at him. "You're what? But you're Italian!" *His profile pics!* Now that I thought about it, maybe his hair was more auburn than brown. How hadn't I noticed before?!

He smiled. "I know, it's a bit rare, but—"

I then whipped out my phone and activated the flashlight mode, dousing him in light like he was a criminal out on the streets. He held up his hands, squinting from the sudden brightness. Under the light, I learned that he was in fact correct. He was a fucking redhead.

I slammed down my phone and shook my head. "Great. I guess we can *never* do anything outside during the day."

If he was offended by this, he didn't show it. Maybe that was my initial draw to redheads: they are rarely ever offended by anything. I sincerely think they are devoid of emotion. That's all dandy, until you go on a roller coaster with one and his expression literally doesn't change the whole time. That's just wrong.

The Italian looked a whole lot like Seth Green. However, because I'm an asshole, I kept calling him "Seth Rogen" the whole night. He sort-of found this funny.

After about an hour of easy conversation, I excused myself to the bathroom. It's important to note this was one of my first official dates after the divorce. I wanted things to go well. I even dressed up, which plainly means I wore high heels with my jeans. (I spend my days in yoga pants and flip-flops. That's my uniform.)

I'm trotting to the bathroom confidently when my heel

grazes across the bar's overly waxed floor, and I slip, landing straight on my ass in front of the whole bar. I know Rogen saw this. Everyone had seen my blunder.

A waiter rushed over and helped me up, asking if I was all right.

"I'm not drunk," I said in a rush, speeding off for the restroom before anyone else could talk to me.

If there had been a back exit by the bathrooms, I would have taken it and never looked back. There wasn't, though. I checked.

In the bathroom, I stared down at the devices of my demise. Fucking hooker shoe! Damn, karma was a bitch!

I thought about taking the torture devices off and strolling out of the bathroom all good-naturedly. However, momma taught me right. *'You always wear shoes in a fancy place.'*

Carefully, I returned to the table, taking each step like I was walking across a tightrope. The floor was like the surface of a fucking swamp, slippery and dark. I decided to own my fall.

"Are you okay?" Rogen asked when I finally made it to the table, each step slow and tentative.

I smiled and nodded. "Yes, and I guess we've just had our first Fifty Shades of Grey moment," referencing the famous scene when Anastasia slipped in Christian's office upon their first meeting.

He arched a single eyebrow and flashed a sideways grin, not missing a beat. "So when are we having our second Fifty Shades moment?"

I couldn't help but laugh. This dating thing wasn't so

hard if I didn't take myself too seriously. If I fell on my ass, I just had to get back up again.

"Miss, are you okay?" the bartender asked, having come all the way over to check on me. "I saw you fall."

I turned to her, shaking my head. "I promise, I'm not drunk."

"Oh, I know that." She pointed at the awful floor. "Everyone slips on these hardwoods. It happens pretty much nightly."

I scowled at the woman. "That seems like something you should look into, not just casually announce."

Rogen and I dated for several weeks. I'm not going to say I got over the fact that he was a redhead, but since we only saw each other when the sun had gone down, it didn't seem to matter much.

Fun fact: I once spent an entire day with a redhead at a sunny theme park. Six of the twelve hours of that day were spent reapplying sunscreen. Because I'm an asshole, each time we stopped to fetch the sunscreen, I'd report that I still didn't need any. "For some reason, I don't burn," I said as he slathered on the thick, white cream. "I don't even freckle."

The guy, who was three freckles away from looking like he had a full body tan, merely shook his head.

It's painfully difficult to offend a redhead.

One evening, Rogen came over to hang out, a rare occasion when I didn't have my daughter. Even still, I reserve a lot of the time I don't have Eleanor for working.

Rogen was lounging on my couch when he yawned loudly. I didn't immediately worry that he was bored by my company. Instead, I hopped up and clapped my hands, startling him awake. "Hey, looks like you're tired. You'd better leave. Can't sleep here."

And they say it can't be done, but *I* did it! I offended a redhead.

Rogen flashed me an angry look, crossing his arms in front of his chest. "You know, Sarah, you're too much of a loner. As much as I make myself scarce, you're still always looking to get rid of me after a couple of hours." He stood, frustration evident in his expression. "You need someone who is never around. Someone who doesn't mind seeing you rarely. You need to date a pilot."

Chapter Six

SEE YOU NEXT TUESDAY

When I first moved back to Los Angeles after the divorce, I wanted to renovate myself, like an old Victorian house that had withstood the Great Depression. I started running for exercise, knowing that's the best way to burn calories. It's also the best way to get abducted by crazies and bitten by loose dogs.

Before, when I was married and ran at night, someone would know if I didn't come home. However, these days, if I run in the evening and don't come home, no one will know...maybe for days. I live in a fairly safe neighborhood, but no place is perfect. Also, the boy next door to me is a rotten teenager who I don't trust for several reasons, one being that he throws his homemade drug pipes over the fence and onto my patio. Imagine my surprise when Eleanor found one while playing. If I wasn't so afraid of the little monster, I would have chucked it in his face instead of in my trashcan. Later, I realized it had my fingerprints on it and that it will probably come back to haunt me one day when I run for public office.

On one occasion, I was running on the sidewalk, and the neighbor boy dangled his upper half out of his mother's passenger car window as they passed, his arms waving. He yelled like the crazed lunatic that he was, making me nearly jump into a thorny bush. I thought his mom should have prohibited such things, and then realized she wasn't that kind of mother. I'm not judging, I'm just saying we wouldn't be in the same mommy groups.

When I first moved into the townhome, I was loading groceries into the house, and the teenager didn't know I had come back out to the car to get more stuff. He threw down his skateboard and yelled from the patio into his house, "Hey, the puta just got back!"

I've literally never had a conversation with the family next door. They have no reason to loathe me unless it's because my orange tree drops plump, ripe fruit onto their patio for them to enjoy. They refuse to make eye contact with me. I keep waving at them, though, and biting my tongue when they fill up my trash receptacle with beer cans.

My Spanish is not so good, but I still knew that the little fucker was insinuating that I was running a brothel—like I'd do that out of *my own* house. I came around the car right after he finished yelling, and the psychopath just scowled at me, not even a bit embarrassed about being caught calling me a prostitute. And that's one of the main reasons I don't think running on the streets at night by myself is a good idea.

Also, I have a fear of dogs that goes back to being chased by packs of strays when I was a child. They'd always stalk me on the way to the bus stop and, because they were dutiful mutts, they would wait for me to get off the bus in the afternoon. I'd run for my life, throwing bits of my left-over lunch behind me to try and keep them from taking a bite out of my calf.

My mother's method of dealing with this was that she gave me a large walking stick to carry back and forth to the bus stop. She told me to shake it at the dogs and yell.

"Why can't you just take me to school?" I asked, fearful of being mauled. "The dogs growl at me. I'm afraid of them."

"Sarah, you can't run from your problems," my mother answered, and then headed for her room to take her usual afternoon nap. "If the phone rings, I'm not home. Tell the bank I'm at work."

My mother, in all my life, has never worked. Not one single day. She was a southern debutant and is still highly offended that I work for a living instead of striving to marry a surgeon.

Back to the renovation of my ass. Tired of being harassed by my dumbass neighbor, who smokes pot before school every day because he's really going places, and also scared of dogs, because I left my giant walking stick in Texas, I did what any gal would do in my situation. I went and got a shiny membership that I couldn't afford at a fancy Pilates studio.

First off, I don't like to sweat when I work out, and Pilates is perfect for that. Micro-movements and zero cardio ensure my body temperature rarely rises. One day, there was a particularly hard instructor, and I remembered barking at her, "Hey, I don't come here to sweat. If I wanted that, I'd go to Gold's Gym."

"Why do you come here?" she challenged.

I rolled my eyes as I balanced precariously on the reformer machine. "So I can drink wine and eat carbs, obvi."

That wasn't entirely true, but she nodded in agreement. That was why most of the ladies did butt crunches every day—to consume calories. However, the truth was that the yoga classes there are like my church; when I tell really religious people that, they are sort of offended. But also, the workouts are challenging, the people interesting and the fodder never-ending. It's much better working out next to rich socialites than next to sweaty brutes at Gold's Gym. I came to the studio originally for the workouts, but I've been staying for the overheard conversations.

One such conversation happened between two women I eavesdrop on often. One of them probably takes classes just to be able to lift the five-carat monstrosity of a ring on her finger. She's one of those ladies that, from the back, you swear is a smoking hot twenty-something with her long, lush hair and tight ass. Then she turns around, and you realize she's well past menopause. Still hot, just not young.

The ladies, per usual, were discussing their Alo leggings, which they treat like disposable pants, only wearing them once before giving them to the poor. I rotate the same three pairs of yoga pants, not only because I'm cheap, but also because I'm allergic to shopping. I still wear the same clothes I did in high school. Even if I wasn't cheap, there's zero chance I'm shelling out one hundred and twenty dollars on pants unless they'll do Pilates for me.

The hot, old lady turns somber suddenly and shakes her head at her friend. "Chanel isn't doing so well. I fear she's not going to make it much longer."

Chanel, I'd learned from over a year of eavesdropping, was her labradoodle—a mix of Labrador and poodle. I'd considered getting one of the hypoallergenic dogs since they have a good temperament. I reasoned that it might heal me of my dog fears. And as a bonus, I could teach it to attack the neighbor boy when he skateboards dangerously close to my parked Prius. However, the price tag on one of these potentially inbred dogs was a deterrent to this budding idea. Three thousand dollars is the amount I'd pay for a jet ski, not for something that shits on the floor.

"I'm sorry," the lady said consolingly to her friend as we changed the springs on our reformer machine. "You know, after Chanel passes, you could do what I did and have her cloned."

I whipped my head around suddenly. Was I dreaming? Had I been dropped into one of my sci-fi books?

Turns out *no*. I was indeed at the twelve o'clock Pilates class.

"Yeah, I'm considering that," the hot grandma replied to her friend. "And for only fifteen thousand dollars, I think that it would be well worth it. Then Chanel number two and I could start all over from the beginning."

I gulped and looked down at my faded yoga pants. I was too cheap to replace these suckers because the stitching in the crotch was still passable, but these women dropped fifteen grand like it was bus fare. I get that it was for a good enough reason—to side-step death and aging, which they both looked like they'd done with numerous surgeries. Still, that day, I realized how different my classmates were from me. I was the foreign exchange student from a Third World country who had gotten the golden ticket to Eton College.

We were two very different classes of people. They, like Barbara Streisand, cloned their animals to keep them around forever. I was more like John Wayne Gacy, in that I planned to bury my cat in the backyard after he died. Of natural causes, I'd like to add; I'm only like Gacy in burial practices. I can't even kill a rat, but we'll get to that later.

I'm not the only one who can't afford Pilates classes but doesn't let that stop them. My friend Sandra got hooked after I dragged her along to a few sessions.

"Seriously, my legs have totally changed shape," she said to me one day. "I can only imagine how round my butt will be after a few months."

"So you're going to keep going?" I asked, remembering that she was already in a contract with another gym.

"Yeah, I told the other gym that I'm pregnant to get out of the contract."

I shot her a cautious look. "Don't you think that's a bit dangerous?"

She shrugged. "Probably, but it doesn't matter. They say that's not a valid enough reason for getting out of the contract."

"Yeah, you don't want to be one of those fat fake-pregnant women," I said. "Even they are supposed to work out regularly."

"That's why I'm crafting a letter from my doula," Sandra said triumphantly.

"You still have a doula?" I asked, looking across the playground as our elementary school children played.

Sandra smiled. "No, but I made a letterhead for one and wrote up a note that states I'm not to do any exercises."

"Wow, you do get that karma is a bitch?" I asked, remembering how hooker shoes, and the floor I fell on, bit me in the ass. Literally.

"It's fine." Sandra waved me off. "And these jerks are trying to hold me to a dumb contract, even though Franklin gets bored at their childcare."

"Remind me never to cross you," I stated. "You'll go to some pretty impressive levels to get what you want."

"I'll say," Sandra said. "Turns out we really don't have the budget for the monthly membership at the Pilates studio."

"What are you going to do?" I asked.

"Henry thinks he can offload a few bottles of bootlegged whiskey each month," she answered, referring to her husband.

"Wait, you're going to sell bootlegged whiskey to pay for Pilates?" I asked.

She smiled victoriously. "Yeah, it should just be enough to cover it, as long as I can get out of this other contract. Do you have a wheelchair? It would be great if I was in one when I dropped off the letter from the doula."

I shook my head. "No, but just imagine what you could accomplish if you used your powers for good."

My constant exposure to the rich and privileged at the Pilates studio offers me the opportunity to learn about all the trendy LA stuff. Things like goat yoga would have never traveled across my ears if I merely locked myself away, writing all day.

"What exactly is goat yoga?" I asked my yoga instructor, Sammy.

"You do yoga with goats around you," she explained in her airy voice. "Sometimes they jump up on you, offering a gentle massage."

I laughed. "You're kidding, right?"

Her grim expression told me that she was in fact not joking. "It's really good for people who are too self-conscious to try yoga. The goats loosen them up. And as a bonus, a glass of wine is included in the fifty-dollar fee for the session."

I wasn't going to offend Sammy again, who was gentle as a lamb. However, secretly, I was thinking that my kinfolk in Texas probably would have *paid* a tourist to come stretch and exercise with their goats, and thrown in a glass of boxed wine for free.

Most of the ladies at the studio have strange eating habits. Jennifer, one of my instructors, is a vegan who is constantly talking about cashew cheese or these seven-dollar donuts they sell at the health food store next door. My vegan friend explained, when I told him about these outrageously expensive donuts, that it was because nuts are so expensive.

"You mean those shelled things they feed to elephants at the circus?" I asked.

He ignored me, which is what most do when I've made an excellent point they can't argue with, and went on, "Also binding agents are expensive, things like aquafaba and agar agar powder aren't cheap or easy to come by."

I'd done my homework and wasn't going to be defeated by some scrawny vegan. "Right, aquafaba is the cost of a can of beans since it's the juice the legumes are stored in. And agar agar powder is essentially seaweed, that shit that washes up naturally on Malibu beach. How about I go get you some and make you a donut? I'll only charge you five dollars."

I don't think he was too keen on my offer since he politely changed the subject. Vegans are so damn nice with their pleasant demeanors and preservation of all things that are living. That's not how I can spot a vegan, though. I know someone is vegan from the sheer fact that they never shut the fuck up about it.

"There's a really yummy vegan yogurt that is amazing," Jennifer said one day during class.

"What?" I feigned surprise. "You're a vegan? I had no idea."

Over the past few months, I'd heard Jennifer go on incessantly about every substitute for all good things in life from cheese to buffalo wings. Seriously, if you don't think you're missing out on anything, then why is it masquerading around like the real thing? Buffalo cauliflower, meatless hamburgers, crispy vegan smoked-mushroom bacon, tofu chorizo. Why copy these foods? Why not just eat your fruits and veggies if you're not missing anything? Just call it cauliflower or spicy macer-ated tofu? Why grind up mushrooms and form and color it to look like bacon? You vegans aren't missing bacon, *are you?*

Jennifer smiled sweetly at my question. "I thought you knew that I was *exclusively* vegan."

I nodded. "That's right. I forgot." *Because you haven't mentioned it in five minutes,* I thought.

One day, Jennifer was complaining about how her hair was growing too thick and long. My head perked up from the reformer machine. This sounded like my kind of problem. I was instantly curious.

"I think I'm going to have to cut back on the collagen I put in my vegan smoothie," she said, holding up a long strand of hair. "It's just too much."

You poor thing, I thought, wondering if maybe she should call Sally Struthers's children to tell them of her plight.

"My nails are growing so fast, I can't keep up," she continued.

"This collagen?" I asked, not aware that you could ingest this stuff. I thought doctors simply injected it into old women's lips.

"It's great," Jennifer said with a smile. She's super nice, probably because she doesn't eat animal babies like I do. "I'll send you the website."

That night, I followed the link that Jennifer sent me and found a site that sold various forms of collagen peptides. The thing that struck me from the get-go was the source. I searched and searched and found that all sources of collagen are derived from animals. There was literally no way around it.

Jennifer's voice from earlier that day rang in my head, *'I'm exclusively vegan.'*

The English teacher in me wanted to sit the sweet vegan down and teach her the meaning of the word "exclusively."

I decided never to say anything to Jennifer about her failed vegan diet since it would make me look like an asshole. I learned that the hard way one day when I corrected one of the other instructors.

As we held a plank, Pelé told us over the microphone about this woman who'd cut her off in traffic. Pelé, named after a famous soccer player, often tells us colorful stories while we're begging for mercy. The first time we met, I told her that I'd almost named my daughter Pelé.

"What?" she exclaimed. "That's crazy."

"So crazy," I said dryly. "Alas, it wasn't going to work because I couldn't figure out how to get that thing over the 'e.' I gave up in the maternity ward and settled on something I could spell on an American keyboard."

I apparently have a sense of humor that leaves people wondering whether I'm joking or not. It's a gift.

"So this woman has cut me off twice in traffic," Pelé stated, as I nearly started to sweat, my abs quaking from holding plank. "You can come down in three, two, one."

I fell down into child's pose with a *thud*, rolling over on my tailbone in preparation for the next torture exercise.

"Then the woman pulls in beside me at the smoothie shop, parking entirely too close to my car," Pelé continued. "A real See You Next Tuesday."

"A what?" I asked, silently feeling sorry for this woman who suffered from the same spatial dysfunction as me.

"A See You Next Tuesday," Pelé repeated. "You know, it's how we politely call women bad names."

I shook my head. "I don't get it. I happen to like Tuesdays. It's when I have tacos."

She laughed. "No, it's code. You take the first letter in

each word." She cupped her hands to make a "c" and then a "u." "Get it? C-U-N-T. See you next Tuesday."

I nodded like I got it. "Ummm...you do realize that two of those four words don't in fact start with those letters? 'See,' as in 'See you next Tuesday' starts with an 's.' And 'you'..." I trailed away, her blank stare communicating that my spelling lesson was completely unwelcome.

"See you next Tuesday," I said, my voice injected with excitement. "That's brilliant!"

"Isn't it, though?" Pelé said with confidence. "And no one knows that you're secretly calling someone a bad name."

Or that you can't pass a second-grade spelling test, I thought, already making plans to anonymously leave a dictionary in the studio's bathroom.

Chapter Seven

I BELONG TO A CLUB OF OLD MEN

You know how women will say, "Oh, most of my friends are guys."

Well, that's not completely accurate for me. I have a fair share of women friends, but the no-drama type. If you want to argue over petty shit, take your ass to the curb. I don't do drama. However, I also have a large network of guy friends, but not like Ross and Chandler from *Friends*. Oh no, my male friends are older, married, or both. Not gay, mind you. For some reason, gay men are repelled by me. It's the strangest thing, and I've never been able to understand it. It's a bit frustrating, because all I've ever wanted was a gay best friend to help me with my defunct sense of style. Alas, there is no Will for this Grace.

When I was in high school, I was cast for the lead in the school play. My co-star was a redheaded homosexual who studied Wiccan. See? Even then I couldn't get away from the damn redheads. However, Chris wasn't drawn to me like most gingers. Quite the opposite.

In the play, we were a married couple who had to kiss. I'm a professional actress—or at least, back then I thought I was. I was all up for snogging the sweaty warlock, but he wouldn't have it. Whatever it was, he could hardly stand to be on the same stage as me. So when it came time to kiss, he put his palm over his mouth, and I laid my lips on the back of his hand, making it look as real as I could for the audience. After the play was over, Chris apparently put a spell on me.

And that's why gay men don't like me.

One time, I was at a James Blunt concert at the Belasco Theatre in downtown Los Angeles—an intimate setting with a capacity of only sixteen hundred. I didn't realize that my future husband, James, had a big gay following. For that reason alone, I feel like gay men should like me, or at least be able to stand me: we share a common obsession with a British musician. However, they are repelled by me. It's sad.

I was roughly five rows from the stage, a close enough distance that I should have been able to get James' attention, putting my own witchcraft on him so that he knew he was "beautiful" to me. There was only one problem with this clever plan of mine... Well, besides that George and I were married at the time, and he was stationed right next to me. He always dampened my chances to get a rock star boyfriend; like when I was at a private recording for One Republic, and he kept introducing me to everyone as his "wife." *Dude*, how was the lead singer, Ryan Tedder, going to ask me out if I had some label on me?

Don't worry, I was totally loyal, and George knows that. Like any healthy couple, we had an agreement that I could have a pass for James Blunt, Rob Thomas, or other eligible rock stars. Problem was that George always sabotaged my chances by being present.

Anyway, also stationed close by during the James Blunt concert were two giant men—the sweetest couple one ever saw, holding hands and ready to sway to the music. The issue for me though, was that the towering men were directly in front of me, not only blocking any view I'd have of James, but any view I had of anything that wasn't their asses. Seriously, I'm so short that my head was even with their waistlines. Not cool.

Forgetting that Chris had jinxed me all those years ago, I tapped one of the men on the shoulder. Okay, I tried to, but it was more like the small of his back, which was where everything started to go wrong.

When he turned around, he looked out at the crowd behind me, a scowl on his face.

"Down here!" I yelled, like an ant on the ground.

The brute looked down at me like the Jolly Green Giant, except without any cheer or green beans.

"Hey, I can't see from behind you," I sang playfully. "When the show starts, will you hunch down a little?"

Okay, I was kidding obviously. Maybe I was hoping they'd take pity on me and let me in front of them. I seriously don't take up much room.

One of the men laughed, the smaller of the two, because, let's be honest, it was funny. His boyfriend was like an NBA star who'd probably ruined movies for thousands of people with his fat head and broad shoulders.

The smaller man nodded, smiled. "Yeah, we can—"

"I don't think so," the taller man said, cutting off his boyfriend. He then turned around, making his partner do the same.

Their terse words and the giant's angry stares over his shoulder told me I'd crossed into the wrong territory. The curse was still active. *Fuck my life.*

"I've told you before that you should keep your mouth shut," George warned in a whisper. "You're too sassy, people don't always like it."

I ignored him right in time for the shorter man to storm off.

Goliath spun around and yelled in my face. "Look what you've done! You've created a fight!"

Right. It was me. Obviously, I was to be blamed for this. I was the reason that most people were assholes. Just blame it on me.

I really didn't want George to get involved. Which was good, because when I turned around, I saw that he'd taken three giant steps backward. When I turned back around, the obscenely tall, angry man pushed me, making me stumble. I was shocked. Seriously, who pushes someone who is so short, she nearly qualifies for handicapped parking?

I was still disoriented when a few girls came to my rescue. They'd witnessed the whole thing and assured me that the guy had gone from happy to hostile instantly. Yep, the curse was keeping gay men everywhere from liking me.

Thankfully, the women took an instant liking to me and invited me to join them in the third row, close enough that James could fall in love with me. I'm still waiting for him to call and tell me he hasn't gotten me out of his mind, five years later. It *will* happen.

So since gay men have banned me from their friendships, and I've banned catty women from my life, the majority of my friends are old men. Makes perfect sense, right?

When I go to the grocery store, one of the produce guys, Bob, who has a head full of gray hair, always stops what he's doing to come over and greet Eleanor and me. We chat easily, catching up on each other's affairs.

Then there's the wine guy on the other side of the store. You know I'm tight with that guy. He's a seventy-year-old Italian named Giuseppe, who often entertains me with stories of growing up in the Bronx while he helps me pick out a case of wine for the week.

These guys are my friends, and I always look forward to their wide smiles and twinkling eyes. On more than one occasion, one of them has rushed out to my car while I was loading groceries to offer Eleanor and me a complimentary bouquet of flowers. We always beam and tell them how grateful we are for their friendly gift.

Guess what happens when the hot produce guy, who is my age and has green eyes like the waters of Lake Tahoe, says hi to me? If you guessed that I pretend my phone is ringing or that I've just stepped in gum, then you get a thousand points, only good for bragging rights. On more than one occasion, he's smiled at me across the pile of lemons, offering a compliment.

"Would you like a free sample?" he asked one time, holding up a ripe nectarine.

My eyes dropped as my face flushed red. "No, thanks. I don't like fruit," I said, hurrying off, hoping he didn't notice the melon, bag of apples and crate of strawberries in my cart.

Since then, if I see Mr. Green Eyes doing his job, arranging the fruit just right, I veer toward the dairy section.

"Don't we need lemons," Eleanor asked one time I tried to dodge the produce guy.

Damn kids and their fucking questions.

"No, we're good. I'll get the inferior bottled stuff," I muttered to her in reply.

"But you say that stuff—"

"Who wants cookies?" I said in an attempt to get her compliance.

"Me! Me! Me!" she sang.

"Looks like Bob is over there." I pointed. "Get him to help you pick some out."

Since I can't stay out of the produce section forever, I've managed to figure out the days that the hottie produce guy doesn't work, and I go shopping then. Yes, I get that this is counterintuitive to finding eligible men to date; I should be chatting him up every occasion I get. However, as much as my neighbor might think I'm some puta, I'm really a classy woman.

Firstly, I won't flirt with a man when I'm with my daughter. That's just gross. And I can't date anyone who I could casually run into if things don't end well. So men in the following areas are off-limits: the gym, grocery stores, the park, Eleanor's school, my work, and in a five-mile radius of where I live. I call it the *protected zone*. That's an easy rule to follow; it leaves tons of options.

I was at the grocery store one day when I picked out an

onion from the bottom of the artfully arranged pile. In my defense, it was the best-looking one. I had it nearly in the bag when the rest of the pile began to fucking quake like an avalanche of rocks about to thunder down a mountain. I threw down the pristine onion I'd picked, and launched my body up against the dozens of onions rolling for the floor. Several escaped past my short arms, but by pressing myself up against the shelf of onions, I served as a wall, keeping many of them from busting to the ground like their brethren.

"Did you pull from the bottom?" a voice asked at my back in a sing-song voice.

Fuck my life. I turned to find Lake Tahoe Eyes staring at me with a sideways grin, his arms crossed in front of his chest.

"It was the best one," I said, looking down to see that I was waist-deep in onions. The vegetable of romance.

I pushed them forward, catching a couple as I tried to back away. On the ground, several onions had split open, their pungent aroma wafting through the air.

The guy dashed forward, helping to catch many of the onions as they sought to spill over the side, a vegetable suicide attempt.

"I-I-I'm sorry," I stammered, backing away, picking up pieces of onion before I tripped on them.

"It's fine," the guy said, laughing at me... not *with* me. I wasn't laughing. "I haven't seen you in a while. How's everything going?"

If you're thinking this makes for a wonderful icebreaker, you're absolutely right. We met because I made an avalanche of onions rain down all over the grocery store floor. That would be a great story to tell people when they ask how we met. Unfortunately, that won't be *our* story, since I pretended that I'd lost Eleanor and excused myself. The truth was that Eleanor was with her father, and the only thing I'd lost was my dignity.

"You realize you're never going to meet anyone if you don't actually get out," my friend Alissa said one day after listening to my onion story.

"I get out!" I argued.

"You go to the dog park in the evening and hang out with a bunch of old men," she countered. "And you don't even *have* a dog."

"I'm dog shopping," I stated. "It's like hanging out at a car dealership before the big purchase."

I had developed this strange habit of going down to the park in the evening with Eleanor. At first, it was an attempt to deal with my dog fear. Then I made friends with the dogs, and then their owners. A club of old men met there every evening who mostly had Labradoodles. Eleanor played with the canines, and I chatted with my friends who were all about my father's age.

The running joke was, "Sarah, which one of these dogs are yours?"

"Shush it," I usually scolded my friends. "I'm browsing. I'm going to get a dog as soon as I steal and pawn your jet ski."

A few weeks would go by, and then one of the guys would say, "Hey, Sarah, when are you getting that dog you've been talking about?"

I'd throw the ball for one of the shaggy Labradoodles

and roll my eyes at "the guys." "Why get a dog and have the expense when I can play with yours?"

Alisa shook her head at me as we strolled through my neighborhood, discussing the strange dog club I'd snuck into. "I think you have to get out more—like out of your element. Or you're going to have to get rid of the protected zone."

I gawked at her. "I can't deal in my own neighborhood."

She laughed at me. "It's called 'dating.' You're not 'dealing.' And didn't you say there was a nice eligible bachelor at the park who taught Eleanor how to throw a ball?"

I gulped. Blushed. "Yes, he used physics to teach her how to throw properly. It was so hot."

"Oh my God! You're the biggest dork in the world." She nudged me. "You should take down the protected zone and talk to him, like really talk to him."

"But if things didn't work out, we'd see each other at the park all the time!" I argued, my mouth popping open from a different thought. "What if we had to split the park? Like a strange custody agreement? What if he got the side where the summer concerts happen? What if I got the shitty side where the baseball fields are? There's nothing to do over there. And the guys all meet in the open area."

"Guys? You mean elderly men?" She shook her head. "And besides, what if it works out, and this guy doesn't have to commute, like most you've dated?"

I let out an exasperated breath, my mind already racing through the outcomes of this relationship that hadn't even happened yet.

"Maybe you have walls that are too high," Alisa continued. "How is anyone ever going to get in if you don't let down the drawbridge?"

I grimaced at her horrible and disgusting analogy. "Leave the words to me, Alisa. You suck at them." And yet, I wasn't going to admit that she'd made an excellent point, one I maybe couldn't argue with.

Chapter Eight

I PUT ON PANTS FOR THIS

Since I work from home, most days, dress code is optional. Let's be honest: most days, pants are optional. I'm civilized enough to throw on a pair of yoga pants, a sports top and flip-flops to take Eleanor to school. In the three months of coolish temperatures we have here in LA, aka winter, I exchange my flip-flops for Ugg boots and add a hoodie to the mix. That's about as much diversity as my wardrobe gets. And because I'm a pansy ass, I start shivering when the temperature drops to around sixty degrees. I get that in other parts of the United States it gets much colder, but it's all about what you're acclimated to.

One day when I was getting ready to take Eleanor to a playdate, she burst into my room and said, "Mommy, can you wear *real* clothes today?"

I held up the faded T-shirt I was about to swap for my sports top. "I'm putting *this* on."

She shook her head. "No, can you wear something besides yoga pants and a T-shirt?"

We're going to play at the fucking park, right? The playdate hasn't changed to Malibu Wines without me knowing, right? At Malibu Wines, the guys all dressed in starched khakis with their collars popped, and the girls wore poufy skirts and too much lip gloss. Everyone's too cool for school.

"Sweetie, I like how I dress," I countered. "It's comfortable and fits my personality."

Eleanor slumped with defeat. I'm absolutely certain that the universe gave me a child the exact opposite of me, not to challenge me in every way, but to try and save my horrible lack of fashion. As mentioned previously, I'm a tomboy. I'm pretty sure I didn't brush my hair for a solid three years growing up, and there was maybe six months when I wore the same two T-shirts in rotation.

I *did* have a small stint in high school, when I was obsessed with *Clueless*, that I wore "preppy" clothes. However, for the most part, I've only ever worn jeans and faded T-shirts. And since becoming a full-time writer, my dressing habits have slacked even more, if that were at all possible.

Eleanor, in contrast, was born clinging to pink, frilly dresses. Accessorizing is just second nature to her. I've seen the girl spend an hour constructing an outfit with the same focus that a rocket scientist gives to creating a spacecraft. She disappears into her room and exits looking like Punky Brewster—there's another timely reference.

Every now and then, I do try and surprise my daughter by throwing on a dress, but keep in mind she's worth the effort. Dressing up for men, that's another story.

On the weekends I don't have her, I elect to wear pajama shorts straight after I get home from yoga. Then I lock myself away for two days, alternating between writing and binge-watching Netflix.

Well, that *was* the schedule, until I started this damn dating app.

One Friday night, one of the guys I'd matched with messaged me back. I'd taken Alisa's advice and kept my initial messages to the guys brief. *'Hey, how are you?'* was all I put most of the time.

It shocked me that this actually worked. I hadn't told them anything about me, or described the reasons that I'd decided to swipe right on them, or explained anything about my moral philosophy. Yet, strangely, men responded to this 'Hey, how are you?' approach like it was at all a sufficient first communication.

The guy immediately asked me out to a movie *that* night. It was seven-fucking-o'clock. I looked down at my attire. I had on my pajama shorts. I was binge-watching *The Office* because, for some strange reason, I'd forgotten how Pam and Jim got together, then I got hooked yet again. I couldn't go outside that night! And dammit! Who was this person who wanted to watch a movie at ten o'clock? Didn't he know I'd be snoozing on my couch at that time, one leg over the armrest, and my cat lying on my chest?

I responded as honestly as I could: "I'm already out for the night. How about tomorrow?"

I was sort of 'out.' I was *out* of wine. I was *out* of energy. And I hoped to be *out* like a light soon.

The guy responded within a couple of minutes. "Okay, sounds good. It's a date."

Wait, what? I had a date the next day? My head started to cramp with unease, trying to deal with the fact that I had set myself up to meet a stranger the next day. That entailed way too many things that sounded exhausting. I was going to have to leave my house! I was going to have to drink in public! I might even have to fucking parallel park my car, depending on where the date was.

It's important to note that, besides not being able to regularly park my car, I also can't parallel park. I never learned how. And I get that it's never too late to try, but it's also never too early to throw in the towel. I don't mind circling the streets of LA looking for a parking spot that I can easily slide into instead of doing some geometric equation to park. And valet is my friend. Yes, I'm giving them tens of dollars to do a relatively easy task, but it saves me from going back to Driver's Ed, which would bring up really awful memories. I still can't talk about the things I did to the Driver's Ed car when I was fifteen.

On Saturday night, the night of the date, I put on pants, combed my hair, and followed a YouTube video on how to put on eyeshadow without looking like a Hooker Shoes. Then I drove myself out to North Hollywood, known as 'NoHo' by the locals, aka the pretentious hipsters.

On the way to the restaurant, I called my friend Zoe. We had a rule that I was to tell her where my dates were, just in case the guy turned out to be an axe murderer.

"He's an actor in North Hollywood," I said over the Bluetooth in my car as I drove. "I sent you his profile."

"Yeah, I see it now," she answered back. "I'm trying to figure out where this red-carpet event was in his pics."

It's important to note that every goddamn person in LA has a profile pic of them at some red-carpet event. Okay, yes I'm exaggerating. I, of course, don't have one because

I've never been on the red carpet, unless the hostess area inside Red Robin counts.

"I'm not sure," I said, weaving in and out of traffic. "Maybe it was for a movie he was in."

"Yeah, maybe," Zoe replied, not sounding so sure.

"What?" I asked, sensing her reluctant tone.

"I only wonder what restaurant he works at," she said.

"Oh, come on," I argued. "He seems nice. Last night, he wanted to take me to a late night movie in Santa Monica."

"Yes, I'm just thinking of all those actors who go to late night showings on a Friday night," she said smugly.

"Well, you just wait," I said, pulling into the valet area. "I'm sure he just wanted to have the average-joe movie experience to see how his face comes across on the big screen."

When I arrived at the restaurant, I was cautious as I strode across the floor, conscious that with each step, I was close to slipping and repeating my last dating experience.

Thankfully, I made it over to Mr. Actor without incident, and he had already found a shared booth. I'm a short girl who prefers average height men. Most guys get a little sassy in their profiles because women swipe left on them if they aren't over six feet tall. I'm the opposite. I want someone just under that mark. However, when Mr. Actor stood up to greet me, and his height didn't change, I did have a moment of shock.

In my hooker shoes, we were the same height. I'm five foot even in bare feet. You do the math.

I put on my best Girl Scout smile and took a seat, noticing that Mr. Actor had a shifty look about him.

He was nervous. It was a first date. I had moved like a

robot across the floor. He was no doubt wondering if I had some muscular issue. Later, I might tell him about Hooker Shoes and karma, and then he'd understand. But that was only if the date went well.

We started off easy enough, talking about our careers. I almost felt a surge of victory when Mr. Actor told me about his agent and his ten years working in Hollywood. I was about to call Zoe and put her on speakerphone.

"So it sounds like you make a comfortable living doing what you love. That's great," I said warmly.

Mr. Actor's face turned to one of vengeance. "I wish. Hollywood just doesn't get me. They want me to conform. They want me to be something I'm not."

I shrank back slightly. "So you *don't* act for a living?"

He shook his head, his eyes narrowed. "I recruit people to screen movies."

"Oh, like *late night movies*?" I asked. "Like *last* night."

He nodded.

"But you love it right?" I asked hopefully. "I mean, as an actor, it's got to be nice to work on the side at something that supports the industry."

He narrowed his brown eyes. "It's the worst. I only get paid if screeners show up, and you know how many people bail out of seeing a movie, even though it's free?"

I was guessing a lot, based on the angry expression on his face.

Thankfully, we moved on to other topics. I wish I could say more pleasant ones. The dude picked at his salad— which he was sour about not having any meat on it, although he didn't order any, and it wasn't listed on the menu—while he told me about how he and his ex-girlfriend met. Perfect first date conversation. I had so many questions about this woman! So glad she was all he could talk about. I learned how they met. How their relationship, full of dysfunction, progressed. And, of course, how they broke up. I didn't have to ask my burning follow-up question, because he supplied the answer on his own, telling me what she was up to now and how much he hoped she'd rot in hell.

"Cool, cool," I said, wishing I could take bigger sips of wine in order to end this date earlier. I'd been smart enough to decline food, which I knew would only drag things out longer.

"So you and your ex-husband? Why did you divorce?" Mr. Actor asked.

I had to give it to the guy, he wanted me to kick him in the balls... hard. However, I'm too mature for that and, much like redheads, I'm hardly ever offended, unless I'm in traffic.

I gave him some canned answer and then relished in the silence that followed. All we had to do was get the check, and then I could go home and binge-watch Michael Scott doing awful things.

"There's something I need to get off my chest," Mr. Actor said, leaning across the table.

Important note: there is *never* anything that one needs to get off their chest on a first date. Okay, I take that back; maybe that you don't have a penis, or are a convicted felon. Everything else can wait for date number two, if you make it to that round.

Mr. Actor tied his hands into his napkin, chewing on his lips. "My brother died last year from a heroin overdose."

I gasped in horror as this poor man relived every second

of his brother's death, telling me EVERY SINGLE DETAIL. It was a sad story. One that I seriously sympathized with him for, having lost my own brother at a young age and very suddenly. However, it is not a story for a first date. Not even a second date. Maybe not even...you get the idea.

I stared at Mr. Actor, not knowing what to say.

Thankfully, he had the good sense to sit back and say, "I think I need therapy."

And there it is. That's exactly what dating is not.

I'm not your therapist. I can't help you with your ex-girlfriend issues or the loss of your brother. And I know we're all connected, but I really don't want to be the ringmaster of someone's circus—not at this stage in my life. I was married to a monkey, and I don't want another one.

I agreed that therapy could help Mr. Actor, and he paid the check and gave me one of those bro hugs, where you pat the other person on the back. We both knew there'd be no second date.

However, as I drove home at nine o'clock on a Saturday night, I wasn't thinking how much I couldn't wait to veg out on the sofa. No, the thought predominating my mind was, *I fucking put on pants for this date.*

My hair was done, something that only happens every fortnight. I was wearing heels, which could be a good or bad thing. I'd watched a YouTube tutorial on how to do my makeup. And most importantly, I was wearing pants.

As I drove back to my house, I had a crazy idea. What if I was bold, courageous and practical? What if I used my time wisely, capitalizing on the fact that I was already dressed for a night on the town, even though my date had gone poorly?

Most of my friends have small children... The other lot of them are old and were already in bed, cuddled up with their Labradoodles. There was no depending on them on that night.

So I made the decision to go to a club all by myself— like a superhero in the dating world.

Chapter Nine

WILL YOU BE MY WING MAN?

Now's a good time to get this out of the way, because it's a major flaw in my character that we will revisit many times over: I'm horrible at turning guys down. It's why I was in a relationship for six years that I should have ended after the first six weeks.

I know I'm an asshole. You know that. Every driver who has ever shared the road with me knows it. However, most of what makes me an asshole is the voice in my head that I keep quiet in polite company. Outwardly, I'm a nice person who is sometimes overly concerned with other's feelings. For instance, if a guy asks me out, I'm going to say yes; it doesn't matter if he's overweight, bald, poor, tattooed, redheaded, or a Republican. There. I think I offended at least half the population with that.

My last serious boyfriend said, "You're my girlfriend now, I've decided."

Notice there wasn't a question there. And although I wasn't opposed to being his girlfriend, it wouldn't have mattered if I was. If I didn't want to be his, I still had no choice, like the women who were considered claimed property back in the day, unable to even vote.

Since I'm into blaming, I'm totally pinning this behavior on my mother, who stayed in a fifteen-year marriage purely out of convenience, even though she despised my stepfather.

Again, I'll offer some of the sage wisdom my mother passed onto me at the young age of thirteen, when I was just starting to explore romantic relationships.

"Sarah, you'd better get this straight now, or you're gonna have a lot of heartache throughout your life," my mother told me one day, a cigarette hanging out of her mouth as she filed her nails. "There's no such thing as romantic love. You go looking for it, and you'll be forever disappointed. There's only practical love. It's what counts in life. It's what pays the bills. It's the only thing worth taking a risk for."

And that's why I'm so fucked up.

So when I was sixteen, and this giant named Skyler asked me out, I said yes. Yes, he had a full sleeve of tattoos, a face full of piercings, listened to Pantera, was overweight, and was considered a bit homely-looking. However, he had a great job. Skyler was a computer genius and had a pleasant enough demeanor (when he wasn't in the mosh pit).

I wanted to say no when he asked to take me out, but I didn't want to hurt his feelings. Who I really wanted to go out with was Joey, the average-sized athlete who was smart and handsome. However, he didn't have a job because he was busy studying to get into an ivy league college. And more importantly, Joey didn't ask me out. My life would look very different right now if he did. I'm not blaming Joey for the fact that I spent six years in a relationship with Skyler, who I was utterly not attracted to...okay, I sort of am.

My mother was thrilled about me dating Skyler because she'd just gotten a divorce and a brand new computer, and needed someone to help her with her AOL email. To this day, she still calls it 'the intermet.' That's what it's for, right? To help you meet eligible doctors?

"Don't you let this one get away," my mother warned me. "Well, unless someone else better comes along."

That's why my mother finally ended her marriage— because something better came along. Not a person, mind you. Some*thing* better. A giant inheritance. Why keep the cow if the dairy just sent you a one-year supply of milk? Well, it should have lasted longer than a year, and also sent me to college, but the fifteen acres around our house needed to be landscaped. We will discuss how my mother spent her and my inheritance another time. Right now, we're talking men, and they're almost as important as money (according to my mother).

It took me years to tell Skyler that I wasn't in love with him. I broke his heart. I still remember seeing him curled up on the carpet in the middle of the living room, sobbing like a giant baby—a giant baby with tattoos and a mohawk. It was awful. To this day, I have a recurring dream that I'm in a relationship with him. The entire time, I'm thinking, *No, no, no! I broke up with you! How did I get back in this relationship?*

And then I wake up, and I'm lying next to my ex-husband and I continue to freak out. *No! I divorced you! What the fuck?*

And then I wake up again, but this time for real, alone in the middle of my queen-sized bed. My subconscious is a fucked-up place that tries to torture me, as you can tell.

It has taken all of my adult life, but I think I'm better at telling men 'no' and putting my feelings first. At least, I'm working on it.

After my horrible date with Mr. Actor, I somehow mustered the courage to go to a nightclub by myself. I was ready for a night out and didn't want to waste my efforts even if I were alone. I found myself at a swanky club where college kids and cougars mingle and dance on the weekend.

Sad fact: the cougars in LA are inbred. I'm not referring to the sixty-year-old women who prey on young college boys. I'm actually referring to the big cats. When the city of LA put the 101 freeway through the county, it intersected the Santa Monica mountains, restricting the breeding territory for big cats of all types, including mountain lions, bobcats and cougars. The result, decades later, is that we have inbred animals.

However, to clarify, the cougars at the clubs aren't inbred, as far as I know. They are probably from a prestigious bloodline, with children as old as the guys they dance with. They have moves like Jennifer Lopez and a rack their ex-husband bought but didn't get to keep in the divorce.

After leaving my car with the valet at the club, I strode up to the bouncer, a wide grin on my face. I flashed him my ID and said, "Tonight, I'm coming to the club by myself."

Not even glancing at my ID—he probably didn't even

need to see it—he nodded. "Good for you, honey. Have a good time."

Wait! Don't I get a fucking gold star? I'd never gone to so much as a restaurant by myself. When I travel for business, I always get takeout and eat in my hotel room while watching House Hunters International. I fucking love that show and need to go on it!

The reason I won't eat alone at a restaurant is that I care about other people's feelings, as hard as that is to believe. I always feel bad when I see someone eating alone, and I don't want others to feel that way when they see me dining by myself. I usually make up a story as to why the people I see are dining solo, and it's never a pleasant one.

Oh, I bet that man's wife died, and this was their favorite restaurant. Oh, my gods! It's probably their fiftieth wedding anniversary, and she died just a few weeks short of it!

I have been tempted to ask the lonely diner if they wanted to join my table, because watching them stir their soup and look around the bustling restaurant was too much for me to bear. Why yes, I've once again made this about me.

Once I was in the club, by myself, I strode through the smoky place, trying not to look as uncomfortable as I felt. Packs of ladies and herds of men stood around, all looking ready to pounce on the prey they stalked.

Usually, if I were with my girlfriends, I would chat with them while people-watching. However, if you don't have someone to talk to while looking at people, you're just considered a gawker.

What did I expect to come out of going to a club by myself, I suddenly wondered, as the unease built in my stomach. Was

I looking for Mr. Right here, amongst the cougars and rich kids? Was I just looking for a good time? But if I wanted that, I could have gone home and downloaded a time management game, which was destined to deliver fun. For some reason, there's nothing more thrilling for me than to play games that have work-simulated tasks with no tangible rewards. I'm sick like that.

As I strode up to the bar, I realized why I was at this club. It was about finding confidence. I'd thrown myself into the deep end, knowing it was overdue. If Hot Produce Guy walked up to me that night, I couldn't just brush him off. I kept telling my girlfriends that the timing wasn't right to talk to a guy, but there was no better place than at a club. They were made for exactly that.

I ordered a glass of wine at the bar because hard liquor, especially tequila, goes straight to my head. Then I wake up in the morning and wonder where the blanket to the hotel bed is and why there is a fistful of Mardi Gras beads on the bedside table. That was in Las Vegas, though, and this book is about how everyone in LA is an asshole, not how everyone in Las Vegas is brain-dead.

"Can I buy that drink for you?" a guy asked beside me.

I looked up, grateful that I was already making friends. Then I deflated inside. I have a type. Everyone does. I've dated men of various shapes and sizes. Brunettes, blonds, redheads. Different races. This guy was definitely not my type. He was good-enough looking, but just not for me.

I smiled meekly. "No thanks. But I'd love to cheers."

There! I'd done it. I'd said no.

Somewhere in the backwoods of Texas, my mother was cursing me, having witnessed me turning down a free drink in her crystal ball. But I didn't want to owe this guy anything—not a conversation, my attention, or anything else. And I also didn't want to give him the wrong impression.

I was taking my power back, even if it seemed like it was in an insignificant way. Money is power; we should never delude ourselves into thinking otherwise.

I lifted my glass, and the guy did the same, and we clinked glasses.

"I came to the club by myself," I reported to him, yelling into his ear to be heard over the loud music.

He nodded. "Yeah, me too."

"But I'm a girl, and I've never come to the club by myself. We come here only in protected packs."

He leaned back, looking me over with a creepy stare. "You must be looking for some action tonight."

I shook my head and gulped my wine. This was harder than I thought. "No, I'm looking to redeem myself after a really bad date earlier tonight."

"Giiiiiirl," he said, "you came to the right place. I can show you a good time. You wanna dance?"

I really didn't. I pressed my lips closed. I didn't have to be nice to everyone who asked me out or asked me to dance. I didn't have to subject myself to unwanted attention just not to hurt someone's feelings. Not understanding that was how I ended up going out with Skyler all those years ago. And why I didn't break up with him sooner. I cared more about preserving his feelings than my own.

"You know what?" I began, "I really don't want to dance, but thanks."

Ha-Hah! I'd said no, and this guy wasn't crying from my

rejection. *This is getting easier.* I looked around the club, which was starting to fill up with people.

The guy finished his drink, not at all looking deterred by my rejection of his offers. "Well, we can just talk. How about I get that next drink of yours?"

I *would* need another glass of wine soon...

"Thanks, but no. What I actually need is your help here."

"Girl, I can help. What do you need?"

A group of guys that *were* my type had entered the club, one of them locking eyes on me.

I took a step back from the guy I was talking to and smiled. "What I need is a wingman. Can you do that for me?"

"Ouch!" the guy cried, shrinking back. "Wingman? I offer to buy you a drink or do whatever it is you need, and you reduce me to wingman immediately. Who does that?"

A part of me wanted to cave. Laugh and tell this guy I was joking. Take him up on his offer to buy me a drink and probably spend the next six years trying to let him down easy.

Instead, though, I pushed my shoulders back and stood taller. "I do that. You're an attractive man, but not right for me. I know what I want, and it's over there." I indicated with my head. "The job is yours if you want it. Be my wingman, and I'll be yours. I'll help you get any honey in this club you desire."

"Except for you, right?" he asked, like double-checking for prosperity's sake. His large brown eyes swelled with hope like I might have changed my mind in the last few seconds.

I hadn't.

"I'm not really available," I said plainly.

Standing up for what I wanted, or in this case, what I didn't want, didn't make me an asshole. It made me a champion to my true desires. Why settle when I could have Joey from high school or the guy on the far side of the club who looked a lot like him?

The guy beside me gave me a curious stare, like trying to figure out what species of strange female I was. "If you're not available, then why are you here?"

"I'm trying to work on it. This is my attempt." I extended a hand to the guy and said, "I'm sort of bad at this. How about you give me some pointers as my wingman?"

"And in return?" he asked, looking skeptical.

I drained my wine glass. "I'll buy *you* a drink."

Chapter Ten

KARMA IS ALSO AWESOME

One day, my ex-boyfriend posted something on Facebook that made me peel back from the computer with unbridled relief that I'd cut that train wreck loose. I then sat back and watched as the mob of angry Facebookers gathered their pitchforks and flaming torches and went after him. I didn't take joy in watching him be roasted, but it solidified my belief that I'd made the right decision when I mustered up the courage to break up with him.

There were a lot of problems with the relationship, which is why I avoided him for weeks until he finally got the hint and broke up with me. That's usually how I deal with problems. Real mature, right? Chiefly, the problem was that our moral compasses pointed in different directions. Okay, let me be honest: I don't think he has one—or maybe it's completely off—but who am I to judge? He is a Taurus, though. Just saying.

He does have many other great qualities. I'm not one to completely put down my exes. I did choose them in the first place, so what does that say about my judgment, if they are horrible people? In this instance, I'll say he's a talented person with flaws, which I uncovered only later and that I couldn't overlook. Still a good person, just not the right one for me.

Somewhere out there, David Tennant is waiting for me to overlook his flaws; like the fact that he can't sleep in and therefore gets up extra early to squeeze me fresh orange juice. And also that he can't stand to finish his frozen yogurt and therefore always gives me that last bite. *And* that he gets bored just watching Netflix and needs something to do with his hands, like rub my feet. Damn you, David! You might be flawed, but I will love you anyway. I will see past your imperfections.

My ex-boyfriend had made a public statement about money that made him look like a power-hungry entrepreneur. This was a quintessential topic where we differed, but he was in finance, so...

I tried to look at this from my profession as an author. Libraries get my books to readers, but I don't make as much as an author. However, I don't need to make a dollar off every book I sell. Scoring the loyalty of the reader is much more valuable. And also, I'm a firm believer in doing what's right because it's the correct thing to do, not to get some reward. Having libraries doesn't just make sense to the Earth, which is wrestling with all our over-consumption, but also makes sense to the community, which needs books from all avenues: ebooks, paperbacks, used paperbacks, and audio. Libraries enrich communities, and more than once, I've been known to leave my paperbacks on the shelves of one of these institutions, hoping it would make it into the rotation of books checked out by readers. I figure my books are like crack. Get them hooked on the first one, and you've got them for life. Yes, I'm a drug dealer.

I am getting to a point, I promise.

The other day, I took Eleanor to Target because I wanted to buy a lot of shit I didn't need. I was about to park when I saw something in the parking space. It may shock you, but I didn't run over the object. Instead, I parked my car perfectly. Apparently, the parking gods were looking down at me.

I got out of the car and looked closer at the object I'd seen when parking: a wallet.

I picked it up, and Eleanor starts yelling, "Don't steal, Mommy! That's not yours!"

I rolled my eyes at my sweet, innocent child as onlookers gave me cautious glares.

"I'm checking to see who this belongs to," I told her.

I held up the wallet to the people around, asking them if they'd lost it.

No one had.

I continued to look through the wallet.

"Why are you going through that?" Eleanor asked.

"I'm trying to see if I can find information on the person who lost it," I said.

"Why not just turn it in to Target?" Eleanor asked.

"Because they are going to simply put it in a lost and found bin and not make any effort to find the person it belongs to."

"So?" my little sociopath said.

"So, if it was my wallet, I'd want to know right away where it was," I explained, reading the guy's ID. "This guy,

Chris So-and-So, could be putting a hold on all his credit cards right now. That's what I'd be doing, and it's a pain in the butt."

Eleanor shrugged, starting to get antsy for our Target shopping spree. I'd promised her we'd buy *The Greatest Showman*—a musical we're absolutely obsessed with—on DVD. We have the choreography down pat.

And if you're wondering if I mean Blu-ray, I do not. I don't know what Blu-ray is. I am the one person who still has a DVD player, and I'm damn proud of it. When I was married to George, he kept asking when we could get rid of it and upgrade. But why upgrade when ancient technology works sort of just fine?

When we divorced, George bought a giant entertainment center with all the bells and whistles. But guess who got to keep the Wii that had all the leveled-up characters? That would be me.

"I think I can find this guy on Facebook," I said, pulling up my phone and searching for the Chris whose wallet I'd found.

Sure enough, Facebook provided a profile for the gentleman immediately. *Damn, social media is either going to be the death of us all, or it will save our very lives.*

I fired off a message to the guy while Eleanor danced to *The Greatest Showman* music in her head.

"What did you say?" she asked as we started for the entrance.

"I told him that I had his wallet, and he'd get it back if he paid me for it."

"Mommy!"

My child doesn't think I'm funny at all. She knows that

mommy writes books that people read for entertainment, but to her, my jokes are lame.

"What did you *really* say to him?" she urged.

"I told him I had his wallet and that I would return it to him," I explained. "He's not far from here—only about thirty minutes away, according to his driver's license."

"But, Mommy," Eleanor began. "We have the dinner party! You're supposed to make a cheeseball."

That's right. One of the reasons I was at Target was to get the secret ingredient for my mother's cheeseball. I have another confession to make: I cannot cook. I once tried to sauté cucumbers, thinking they would end up like squash. They ended up in the garbage.

I seriously loathe my cooking, as does my gourmet friend Samar, although she's sweet about it. I can't tell you how many times I've slaved away at the stove to impress her, only to fall short of her expectations. Samar can throw three ingredients in the Instant Pot with a pinch of curry, and voila, she has a fucking thali platter with twelve different dishes. I just knew if I made my mother's famous cheeseball, I'd finally give her something that would tantalize her taste buds. Then she'd stop encouraging me to "just get frozen stuff from Trader Joe's" on the evenings I hosted the dinner party.

I come from a long line of distinguished southern chefs. My aunt was a chef and editor for Southern Living for years, and my grandmothers apparently created a ton of the most iconic Louisiana recipes, which one of them wrote about in her weekly newspaper column. I, however, have failed on more than one occasion to make white gravy. Do not tell my relatives; their opinion of me will sink even lower. I can just hear them now: *'No wonder she moved to the West Coast. Those people don't even know how to fry chicken properly.'*

Anyway, one of our main objectives at Target that day was to get the secret ingredients for the cheeseball. And socks. How does my kid go through fucking socks like the women at the Pilates studio go through Alo pants?

"We won't be late," I told Eleanor. "Or we will. It doesn't really matter. We have a wallet to return."

She agreed a bit reluctantly, her hopes centered on the cheeseball.

My child doesn't like anything with melted cheese, which is good for my ass. Otherwise, I would have eaten a ton of pizza over her lifetime. For reasons unknown to me, she turns her nose up at pizza, cheeseburgers, and nachos— *which is the gods' way of helping me,* I remind myself every time I wish she'd go halfsies on a plate of quesadillas. However, Eleanor fucking loves my cheeseball. It's the right kind of cheese for her.

I checked my phone again, curious to see if the Chris guy had responded about his wallet. He hadn't. I then waved to the falconer as we strode into Target.

Why yes, I did say that my Target has a falconer. Doesn't yours? He's there every week with his birds, doing his service to keep the pigeons away. This Target is much too civilized to have sharp spikes on the light poles and roof to keep the pests at bay. Instead, they hire a falconer, because how do you keep the seagulls away? You bring in the big birds. By the way, seagulls are fucking assholes. Like the biggest ones in LA. There's one in Malibu who still owes me a fucking turkey sandwich... I was hangry the rest of the day because he stole my lunch.

By the time we'd picked out the secret ingredients for the cheeseball (which, no, I'm not divulging), Wallet Guy hadn't responded.

"Looks like we're driving this wallet over," I said to Eleanor as we loaded into the car.

"But we're not going to have time to prepare for the dinner party," she whined.

"And yet, it will still work out," I explained. "The right thing to do is to return this wallet."

"Do you think he'll give us something in return? Like a reward?"

I shrugged. "It doesn't really matter."

"But we're going to be late for our own party," Eleanor reasoned. "I think it matters."

"There's a law that operates in the universe, baby," I began. "It's called the tenfold law. Whatever you do, good or bad, comes back to you tenfold."

"So if we steal the wallet, then..."

"Bad things will come back to us tenfold," I finished her sentence.

Eleanor gave me a doubtful look from the back seat. "I don't know. How can you know for certain that if you do good or bad, it will come back to you?"

I shrugged. "I just sort of know."

We drove out to Ventura County where the owner of the wallet lived. His teenage son was working on something in the driveway when I pulled up. He was cautious when I asked about his dad, like I was some hussy checking on his whereabouts because he'd stood me up on a date. However, the kid's worries evaporated when I presented the wallet.

"Hey, Father's Day is coming up," I told the boy. "Why

don't you get him a wallet that doesn't fall out of his pocket?"

"Good idea," the kid said, holding up the wallet with a smile.

We returned home with enough time to make the cheeseball and heat up the Trader Joe's appetizers. The dinner party was a success, and for the first time ever, Samar said, "I'm going to need the recipe for this cheeseball. It's simply divine."

Fat chance of that, I thought with glee. I may not have a lot of family loyalty, but I know better than to leak my grandmother's secret recipe. Strange voodoo shit would come back to haunt me.

After everyone had left, Eleanor and I were cleaning up. This is a good time to note that I never have any cash on me. Ever. Like most, I'm too reliant on credit cards. And my daughter... well, she's seven, and I don't give her an allowance yet because I'm "mean" and expect her to earn it by doing more than her regular chores. When she turns eight, I plan to construct a list of tasks I've been putting off for her to do to earn money—shit I totally don't have time for, like dusting the baseboards and alphabetizing the library. Kids who get money for making their beds are learning nothing; you're raising assholes who are going to want a tip for doing their fucking jobs later in life.

Guess what I get for making my bed? Nothing. I simply do it so that the cat won't get his hair all over my sheets. We need to teach intrinsic motivators. Guess what I get for busting my ass and writing a full-length book? Real money. That's how it should be.

So I'd asked Eleanor to go pick up the floor while I finished off the cheeseball.

"Mommy! I think you need to come and see this," Eleanor called from the entryway.

I came over, licking cream cheese off my fingers, to find her pointing at the ground. In front of her was a folded up ten-dollar bill.

"That's weird," I said, texting Samar immediately to ask if she'd lost it.

She hadn't.

"I wonder..." I said, baffled.

Eleanor picked up the folded-up bill and opened it. "Oh, Mommy. I get it! 'Tenfold'! It really is true. The universe really does reward good behavior."

I was suddenly speechless. She was right! I could have tried a hundred ways to convince my child that karma was real and operating in her life, but in a single beautiful and magical act, the universe did it for me.

We still have no idea where the folded up ten-dollar bill came from, but it now resides in a picture frame in our entryway to remind us to always do the right thing. Give away your time, your money, your books, or whatever it is, and it will come back to you. But more importantly, do the right thing because it is the *right thing*, not for a reward.

Chapter Eleven

GUYS WHO RUN HOMELESS SHELTERS ARE THE WORST

I had been on Bumble, swiping, for a couple of months when my faith in humanity began to plummet. I couldn't figure out if all men were morons, if it was just the ones in LA, or just the ones I matched with.

I actually paused my profile for a little while because I just couldn't handle the absurdities. I've recently started it back up, and I'm not sure much has changed over the summer. However, if I'm not dating, then there are no ridiculous stories; believe me, I don't make this shit up. How could I?

Online dating profiles really need to be renamed to "Pretentious outlines of traits." It's POT for short. I was going to add, "Subtle lies I tell about myself," but that's getting to be a bit long. I'm much more likely to swipe right (meaning I approve) on a normal guy with a plain background behind him who lists his general interests, than someone who has six shirtless pictures in his profile and says, "just a bee looking for his honey." Do you know how many times I've thrown up reading dating profiles?

Dear men, if you have more than one picture of you at Burning Man, it's probably not going to work out. And your ex-girlfriend is gorgeous, however, is there a reason you chose that picture of her with her arms around you for one of your six profile pictures? It's not like this is 1990 and you have to go to CVS to get your roll of film developed. Just take another selfie. But please stop taking them in the bathroom. I get that you have abs and want to show them off, but I get confused when I see you with a bunch of urinals behind you. Setting is key, and you're not framed very well in the In and Out Burger bathroom. I do like that you took off your apron, but I don't think the customers would like to know that it's currently hanging off the handle of one of the urinals.

Also, men, if I can't see your hair because in every photo you're wearing a hat, I'm going to assume you're bald. If you're not, take off the hat and snap a selfie.

I won't lie, I will probably swipe right on you if you're pictured with a stack of nachos. It's just the way my mind works. Deep in the recesses of my convoluted brain, I think that if I swipe right on you, I will get some of those nachos —which aren't allowed on the Keto diet, and it's the saddest thing in the world.

Mr. Bumble User, posing with a really cute dog does not increase your chances of me swiping right. However, if you hold a kitten while bare-chested, I might be tempted to give you a shot.

Also, you should know that I'm studying your photos. Pick up your damn underwear off the floor. What, were you raised in a barn? And do your friends know they are in your Bumble photos? Also, if all of your photos are group shots, how do I figure out which one is you? I'm not a fucking detective—and if this is your way of saying you like orgies, then I'm glad I swiped left.

If you're wearing a suit in your profile pictures, I'm going to assume you're more of an adult than me. I'm sure you're a wonderful person, but I'm swiping left simply out of intimidation. My dad wears a suit every day, and I don't want to date him. The tenth Doctor also wears a suit, but with red converse shoes, which means he's not all the way grown up. So if you've got on a suit, show me your shoes.

This really shouldn't have to be pointed out, but if you have a Snapchat filter on every one of your photos, it's going to be a hard no. Also, I don't care that you got your photo taken with Arnold Schwarzenegger. Did you really think that I'd be like, "He's got double chins and crossed eyes, but the one time he met the Terminator... I want some of that"?

If your profile picture is of you at a sporting event, I'm going to have to pass. I'm not judging, it's simply that I know what I like, and sports isn't on that list unless it's women's gymnastics. We all make choices with our profile pictures. They are supposed to tell our story. That's why three of my pictures are of me at Hogwarts. If you don't know what that is, we won't work out. If you love Harry Potter but have only watched the movies, this shit won't work. I get that I have high standards, but so does Elon Musk, and look where that's gotten him.

To the guy who took a family portrait at Costco, I don't even know where to begin. Does your ex-wife know that you have your children in your dating profile? Does she know that you take them to Costco while wearing a suit? Does she know that you're letting little Cindy eat pop tarts? Yes, I saw what was in your cart. Those things are lacking any nutrition. Just saying.

Back to profile pictures. I am trying to help you, men, because many of you really don't know how to capture a picture that doesn't make me want to throw up on my phone. If you're flexing your muscles in a race car, we're going to go our separate ways. We have zero in common. I never want to go to a NASCAR event for as long as I live. I'll only make you resentful that I can't stand your hobby, and I'll harass you about how much gas your muscle car wastes. You see how this will only lead to you turning into an alcoholic in an attempt to get away from my incessant nagging.

To the guy who is a giant, towering over all his friends in his photos: I'm sorry, this is just not going to work. I know women like tall men, but I can't date someone who towers too high over me. It will give me issues. I'll always fear you're going to topple over onto me. I quit growing at age twelve, and although I keep taking my vitamins, I fear I'm never going to resume growing. Maybe if my mother hadn't smoked through her pregnancy, I'd be tall like Heidi Klum. It's fine. I've come to terms with it. I like being short; I'm comfortable on airplanes. Take your extra legroom back, I don't need it. Because I'm an asshole, I like to stretch out next to the tall person beside me on the airplane and complain that I have too much room. Meanwhile, their knees are bumping against the seat in front of them, and they have a sour expression on their face. I kick my legs gleefully, my feet not even touching the ground.

If your profile pictures are all of you with sunglasses on, then I'm assuming you're a serial killer. I get that it's sunny in LA, but if I can't see your eyes, it's a no-go, psycho. Also, if you have a cigarette behind your ear in your picture, that's a hard no. Back in 1997, I would have found it cool that you had a Marlboro hanging out in the wings, ready to be smoked, but that girl also used to get high and watch the *Wizard of Oz* while listening to Pink Floyd's *Dark Side of the Moon*. So I don't really trust her judgment.

If your photos pass the test, then I'm going to move onto your bio. Please have a bio. You can't coast by with your good looks and winning smile forever. I don't need your life story, but tell me something that I can use to start a conversation with. And keep in mind that I am grading you on grammar and punctuation. Extra bonus points for following capitalization rules.

This is when I'm going to sound like an asshole. I know, you're shocked. *This* is the moment. I'm so shallow that I will swipe left simply based on a guy's name. There, I said it. I'm sorry, but it's sort of non-negotiable. If I can't pronounce your name, it's probably not going to work out. To Sieb, Piotr, Abdeslam, Efstathio, and Zurab, you all seem like really nice people, but I can't roll my 'r's, and honestly, I still don't know how to read using phonetics. I've memorized every single word I know, and it's unlikely that I'm going to learn any new ones. But note that it isn't you. It's me. I'm an unwilling jerk.

Also, to the Garys of the world, I'm sorry, but we have no future. I just can't take a guy named Gary seriously. Your

name just rhymes with too many things: berry, dairy, merry...
You get the point, right?

I actually dated a guy for a little while whose profile
name was Gary. I was about to swipe left on him when
something in his bio caught my attention. The first line
said, "My name isn't Gary."

I was like, "What?"

We matched, and I told him he nearly got axed because
of the name Gary. He explained that he was using a fake
Facebook account for his profile. That should have been the
red flag for me, but I'm sort of dumb when it comes to
picking these things up. Anyway, things didn't work out
with "Not Gary" because he was one of those guys who has
several fake accounts. Maybe a real Gary wouldn't be so
shifty. I'm not sure.

This is not your fault, but if you share the same name as
any of my exes, it's an automatic no. The list is sort of long,
so that pretty much knocks out half you guys. Sorry.

I also will not date you if your name is an adjective or
verb. Sorry Rusty and Dusty, but your parents named you
after dirty, messed up stuff. That's on them, not me. And to
Tug, Skip and Pat... well, I really shouldn't have to explain
this, so I'm not going to.

If your parents didn't have the good sense to give you
the traditional spelling of a common name, I really don't
think it will work out. I will get drunk on mimosas at Easter
brunch and tell your mother that she fucked up your life,
Khris. It really is inevitable. No one spells your name right,
and it really is her fault.

Oh and Je, your mom forgot to finish spelling
your name.

To Blaine, Ashley, and Preston, no. Just no. Your names mean you were born with a polo sweater tied around your shoulders. We'll never be able to relate, and you know that.

Also, if you're Hispanic but look Asian, I might have reservations. The reverse is true as well. Honestly, I don't think I'm dating any Asians or Hispanics this year, because I have my heart set on going as Rose and the Doctor for Halloween. I'm Rose, so you have to have David Tennant's amazing hair. Oh, and not be Asian. Preferably, you're British or can do an accent as you hold your sonic screwdriver. That was not an innuendo. Okay, I'm lying. That totally was.

Onto the bios. If you state that you're a vegan, I'm probably swiping left. It's not that I'm closed-minded. It's that steak and mashed potatoes are my favorite thing ever. You not being able to share that pleasure with me will create a wedge over time. Also, the only thing I can make well is a cheeseball, so you can see how that's not going to work. And, dammit, I'm not making the famous cheeseball with cashew cheese! My grandmother will haunt me.

After I match with a guy who has passed all of these profile qualifications, it's up to me to respond. That's where things get tricky for me. When responding to guys, I take the same casual, sarcastic tone in my prose that you find here. It helps to weed out the ones who take themselves too seriously or won't be able to handle my dry sense of humor. However, according to my friends—who, by the way, are assholes too—I can be sort of a jerk. Call it a defense mechanism.

I was once at a bar with my asshole friend, Cheryl, the one who told me that I shouldn't describe myself as a science fiction writer. Good lesson to pass onto our children. *'Eleanor, don't describe yourself as you are. Instead, come up with something that won't frighten people away. That will ensure you are attracting people who won't like you for who you are, and that's key.'*

Accountants, for instance, should never introduce themselves like that. To all the accountants out there, here's a word of advice: When people ask you what you do, say you're a zookeeper. Everyone fucking loves a zookeeper. No one likes accountants. It's programmed into our DNA. When people ask you follow-up questions, invite them to pet your monkey sometime. You see how this conversation is going far better already than if you said, "I'm an accountant." There are no follow-up questions to that statement, only sadness and awkward silence.

Anyway, Cheryl and I were at a bar, and these Australian hockey players come over to chat. I think I've mentioned that hockey is on my list of hard 'no's. I like good teeth and, let's be honest, Mr. Hockey is not going to keep his shining smile for long. It's inevitable.

The guys asked if they could sit down, but I'd already learned that they play hockey, so I said no. They laughed and took a seat anyway. One of the guys was six foot six inches and stationed so close that, again, I had that fear he was going to topple over on me. I scooted my chair back and gave him a scolding look.

"Why did you do that?" he asked. "I can't talk to you way over there."

I could have been polite, but I'd had too much wine for that, so instead, I said, "You're too tall. We can't talk."

Because men love an asshole, he laughed, maybe

thinking I was joking. "Would you like to play Jenga with me?" He pointed at the giant Jenga set in the corner.

I shook my head. "I don't play games with tall people. They always win."

He narrowed his eyes at me. "I'm sorry, have I done something to offend you?"

I rolled my eyes. "I thought that was obvious."

Cheryl then gave me a disapproving look. "Sarah, he doesn't know that you're joking and this is just your dry wit."

I shot her a look. "Am I joking?"

She laughed because she's my friend and has learned never to take me seriously. But Mr. Hockey and I weren't destined to be friends for many reasons. By the end of the night, he said I was the meanest person he'd met. Apparently, he didn't like my jokes about how tall people take up too much room and aren't economical, and how we should start breeding short people for downsizing purposes.

It is at this point that I should start making some apologies to guys. I'll start with Mr. Hockey. I'm sorry that you don't have a sense of humor, and that you have to duck when you enter a room. I realize you were trying to hit on me, but I was only trying to save you time and trouble. Your feet would hang off the end of my bed, and then my cat would end up scratching your toes. I was clearly looking out for you by being rude. You're welcome.

To the guy who was holding a kangaroo in his profile picture: I'm sorry I said your dog looked strange. I'm an asshole.

To the guy who had red eyes in his profile picture, I'm sorry I asked if you were a robot. In my fictional world, robot boyfriends are real and pretty amazing. I'm obviously an asshole for insinuating that you were bits of metal, since you deleted me.

To the guy who put that he runs a homeless shelter in his profile, I'm sorry I asked if announcing that got you laid a lot. I'm sure that it's the first sentence in your profile because your altruistic spirit is flooding out of you, and you can't keep your good deeds to yourself. I'm sorry. I'm an asshole.

To the guy who was trying to be cute and said he'd once rescued a drowning puppy, I apologize for telling you that I actually rescued a real puppy who later died from internal bleeding. I realize that killed the romance and that's why you deleted me. I'm an asshole.

To the guy who described himself as a writer, I'm sorry that when I found out you only blog, I said, "Oh, I write *actual* books." I'm sorry. I'm an asshole.

To the guy who sent me his picture before he went into surgery, I'm sorry for only responding with a thumbs-up. In truth, though, I thought it was a little soon in our relationship for pre-op photos. I sort of apologize. Glad you didn't die.

To the guy who deleted me after I said I spend most of my free time with my daughter, *you're* a damn asshole. I'm sorry your momma didn't teach you right.

To the guy who said he wanted to become an acupuncturist so he could put his hands on my body, you're an idiot. That's not how acupuncture works, but I feel like explaining it to you wouldn't do either of us any good. You're an asshole. And no, your come-on didn't make me giggle like a schoolgirl, you creep. I'm sorry we share the same county.

To the guy who asked for my number and then immediately deleted me after I gave it to him, don't sell my shit, asshole.

If there can be any takeaways from this, it should be that profiles need to be created with great care. You're selling yourself to your future wife or lifelong partner or live-in girlfriend, depending on what you're looking for. Also, the initial interactions are key. I'm sorry that I haven't always been perfect with my pickup lines, but I was trying.

And to the guys who have been dicks from the get-go, there's something you should know: I'm an author who crafts villains. If you piss me off, I will name the bad guys after you. I will model them after your bad behavior, and then I will kill them off—painfully.

Chapter Twelve

OBAMA IS UNDER MY BED

It will come as no surprise that my friends are all assholes. I like my friends colorful, with a rebellious edge to them. I can proudly say that I have intelligent, creative and hilarious friends. They are also complete pains in the ass with lots of first world problems.

My friend Matt once wrote a letter to the Buffalo Wild Wings corporate office because they discontinued his favorite sauce. Matt isn't a fat guy who sweats on his sofa while playing video games. He's a high-powered executive who I thought had a busy schedule. Apparently, he has time to write letters. Most of my asshole friends are civilized like that.

I said to him, "You literally have time to write a letter about this situation?"

"Sarah, it's my favorite sauce."

"But it is *just* sauce, you realize that? I thought you wrote letters when schools were cutting funding, or when a pedophile moved into the neighborhood. I didn't think spicy buffalo sauce was worthy of a formal letter."

"You have obviously never had *this* sauce," Matt said, rolling his eyes at me.

My friend Roberto wrote a letter to the grocery store co-op because they changed the cleaning chemicals they used to mop the floor. My running joke with Roberto every time he has a small issue is, "Why don't you write a letter about it?"

My friend Zoe wrote a letter to Michael's craft store because they allowed nonservice animals to stroll around the aisle with their owners. I don't care much about buffalo sauce or cleaning chemicals, but I can get behind this complaint. I get that Rover shouldn't be left in the hot car while you're picking out scrapbooking materials... Guess where Rover should be? At fucking home. Leave him there, and then I don't have to relive my dog issues while I'm shopping for glue sticks. What if I brought my cat to the store with me? Everyone would immediately start sneezing and complaining. Or how about my pet snake? I don't have a pet snake, but what if I did and I carried Mr. Boa around the store? Totally not cool. So leave your dog at home; unless you own the business. Like my Pilates studio. They have a dog, but it's sort of different if you are the boss.

Zoe keeps telling me that I should make an anonymous complaint when I tell her about issues. I halted one day when we were walking and looked at her. "What is this method of making anonymous complaints? Do I cut out letters from magazines and paste them on a piece of paper, all like *Murder She Wrote?*"

"Do you ever make references from this century?" she asked.

I shook my head. "Rarely."

After hearing of my friend's experiences, I've concluded that writing letters is completely ineffective. The sauce hasn't come back, the chemicals still burn Roberto's nose, and if some diva wants to bring her purse dog into Michael's, she's probably getting away with it. There's a sign on the entrance of Trader Joe's, my favorite place on Earth, that says, "Only Service Animals Allowed," but does that deter the lady with a rat-dog? Of course, it doesn't. But I'm not saying anything because, again, Trader Joe's is my favorite place, and I'm not making any enemies there. People like dogs, and if I make a case against them, then they'll figure out I'm a cat person, and no one will like me then.

Since my friends are all pretentious assholes, I have to mess with them. Back in 2008, I volunteered on the Barack Obama campaign. I grew up in politics, in a way. My mother was a very active Democrat who constantly brought me along with her to rallies and campaign events. I met Michael Dukakis, the 1988 presidential candidate, when I was five years old. I still remember him kneeling and shaking my hand.

"I have a granddaughter your age," he said, and I swore he looked into my soul.

I knew about these politicians. They were all-powerful. They knew that which we didn't want them to know. They were fucking Santa Claus.

I looked at the potential next president of the United

States and said, "How do you know how old I am?" Then I yanked my hand from his and stomped off.

I didn't realize then that he was estimating my age. I didn't know that I was being a jerk. I was, as I would continue to be, confused.

My mother thought it was funny; when you're a child, your behavior is usually seen as cute. Thankfully I wasn't a jerk to Bill and Hillary Clinton when I greeted them and the Gores during their campaign. I wore my "Yellow Dog Democrat" pen while I campaigned for them, blanketing the Walmart parking lot with propaganda. Yes, it's probably wrong to make children work in politics, about like forcing religion on innocent minds.

And just like that, I've brought up the two most controversial topics: Religion and politics.

Anyway, it is in my blood to support presidential campaigns. My earliest memories involve lying on a dirty floor, coloring during the Democratic caucus.

In 2008, I spent almost a year of lunch breaks making calls for the Obama campaigns. My colleagues, inspired by my patriotic spirit, decided to get me a prize when Obama was elected as President of the United States. They had delivered to my office a life-sized cardboard figure of Obama. It's totally life-like. Besides my Tardis, Obama is my favorite gift that I've ever received.

The strange thing about my Obama is that he has white hands and no wedding ring. His head was obviously photoshopped onto his body, but I love him just the same. Oh, also the funny thing is that I use him to torture my asshole friends.

When someone comes over to my house, I wait until

they use the restroom, and then I haul ass upstairs, grab Obama from his place under my bed, and set him up right outside the bathroom door. When my unsuspecting guest comes out of the bathroom, they are always frightened by Obama towering right outside the door.

"Oh my gods!" my friend Sabrina said, clapping her hand to her chest. "That scared the shit out of me." She pointed at the very life-like figure of Obama.

"Why? Why does a confident black man scare you?" I teased.

Sabrina moved the cardboard figure out of her way, to the corner of the room. An hour later, she made me put him back in his spot under my bed. "Even though I know he's there, I still keep catching him out of the corner of my eye, and he spooks me."

"Because he's black?" I fired at her.

She shook her head, used to my antics. "He's just creepy. It's like he's watching us."

"He's a politician. Of course, he's watching us."

I have to admit that there is something about Obama's wide smile and twinkling eyes that sort of creeps me out too. Even when I know that he's "out," I still get caught off guard by his presence.

"Dammit, Obama!" I once yelled in the empty house, having come around the corner to find him lurking. I grabbed my chest from fright and shook my head at him. "You get me every fucking time."

Eleanor thinks it's funny to leave rubber snakes around for me to find. I know there is no way that a giant cobra should be lounging on my driver's seat. However, for some reason, I still screamed when I opened my car door one day to find the rubber toy.

That's why I stationed Obama at the bottom of the stairs one day and called her down to the living room.

That little squeal of fear when she spotted Obama was sweet, sweet vengeance.

I've been known to put Obama out for all sorts of people, not just guests. When I moved to Central California, I set him up in the bedroom closet with the doors slightly ajar. Then I waited for the movers to bring in the furniture. Making grown men scream with fear gives my life meaning. The electrician nearly punched Obama in the face when he opened the closet to find him lurking in the dark.

Needless to say, Obama has gotten a lot of use over the years. The cat actually started chewing on him under the bed. What can I say? Everyone loves Obama. I didn't know this mutilation was going on until I pulled him out for a dinner party. He always makes an appearance at my dinner parties. My friend Matt was so delighted to get pictures with the president for his Instagram. It seriously looks like they are casually discussing global warming over the fondue pot.

Anyway, imagine how devastated I was one day to discover that Obama had shrunk two inches and was missing part of his ear thanks to my damn cat. It was like a member of the family had taken ill. I patched him up the best I could and propped him in the corner, since his stand was totally broken.

My friends, who are awesome as well as assholes, came to the rescue. Days later, a second Obama was delivered to the house, courtesy of Etsy.com. Now I have not just one, but two Obamas. The new one is older, gray-haired and just as frightening to unsuspecting guests.

Because I can't trust my cat not to eat Obama, I keep the new one in a case in my closet. When I get dressed, I have to yank my clothes from my closet at lightning speed and then shut the doors before the fucking feline wakes up. Every fucking time I open the closet, it doesn't matter where the cat is in the house, he sprints for the closet, hoping to make it before I close the door. He just won't be happy until he takes a bite out of Obama.

I have found tons of uses for my trusty cardboard figure. For instance, as I've previously mentioned, my next-door neighbors scare me. It's not just the disgusting teenager who creeps me out, but also the shifty drug dealers who drop by at all hours of the night. The front yard is littered with trash, and there's a giant X beside the front door. Real fucking curb appeal.

When I first moved in next to them, I thought about getting a security system; however, let's be honest, I'm too cheap to get Brinks. Also, I'd obviously set the system off on accident, ensuring that the local police became entirely frustrated by my false alarms. And who needs a security system when I have Obama, the cardboard figure who frightens burly movers and my asshole friends?

The neighbors thought that I lived alone with my daughter. They obviously thought they could bully me and I'd never say anything. They were right. But strangely, they quit filling up my trash can and stealing my newspapers when Obama started making an appearance in my window.

At night, I would set him up in the upstairs window with just enough lighting behind him that his features weren't real clear. It comforted me to know that he was looking out on the neighborhood, protecting me more effectively than a security system.

When the jerks next door started crawling over my fence to destroy my yard, I knew Obama had to be put into action. The fuckers were pissed because I'd finally mustered up enough courage to complain about their dog barking all damn day long. I work from home. Writing books takes concentration. Their yelping dog kept me from writing for almost a week.

Also, because my neighbors are such gentle souls, they would walk their dog, use a baggy to pick up its shit, and then launch the bag up onto the community carport. For six months, I looked out my office window to see piles of shit littering the roof of the carport. I have a nice view of the Santa Monica mountains from my office, but strangely, it's hard to appreciate that when steaming bags of shit are dominating the foreground.

After the backyard incidents, I set Obama up downstairs in a precarious place between the drapes. It absolutely looked like a tall man was scanning his backyard for trespassers. Since then, the assholes next door have left me alone. They may never see my giant boyfriend leave my place, but the evidence is clear that he resides in my house. I sleep peacefully at night now with Obama standing guard. We all need a strong, black man in our lives, keeping us safe.

Chapter Thirteen

I HAD DINNER WITH JERRY O'CONNELL

I've had dinner with many, many celebrities. It's a perk of living in Los Angeles. Hollywood is down the "street" from my house and always bursting with movie stars and pop stars. It's not uncommon to be hanging out at a coffee shop in Sherman Oaks while a reality television show is being taped on the street outside.

I don't really watch television that much. I know. I'm one of those people. I see the looks I get at parties when everyone is talking about *Orange is the New Black*, and I say, "I haven't seen the show. I don't watch television." It's like saying I don't pet dogs. It's un-American. It's unpatriotic to not eat frozen yogurt and binge-watch Netflix in the evening. I have been working on this problem of mine.

I recently put down a book and watched *Stranger Things* in the evenings. Then my Netflix got all messed up because George realized I was still using his account and kicked me off. Really rude. It took me a solid hour to figure out how to get my own account using my Wii. Yes, I get that Wii is outdated technology. I literally have no idea how to connect my television to the outside world otherwise. I simply don't know what the options are. Do I get a special antenna? Is there a box that makes the Netflix magically appear on the screen?

Because I live in a cave and don't watch celebrity news or anything trendy, I often don't know when I've just encountered a celebrity. Usually, my friends have to tell me. I was at an Italian restaurant with a friend when she kicked me under the table.

"Fuck! That hurt," I complained. "Why did you do that?"

Alissa leaned down low, a conspiratorial glint in her eyes. "Behind you..."

I did what anyone would do and turned around.

"No," she hissed, grabbing my hand to stop me. "Don't look."

"You said 'behind you,' and I feared an axe murderer was about to cut me," I said. "And also, you've got a crazy look on your face, like you've just seen a ghost or an axe murderer ghost."

She shook her head, her eyes focused on someone at my back. "Kendall Jenner is at the table behind you."

I leaned down low, matching her stance. "Is this Kendall Jenner an axe murderer? Should I be concerned?"

Alissa sighed. Rolled her eyes. "Damn it, Sarah, how do you not know who Kendall Jenner is?"

"I don't watch television," I stated.

"You don't have to watch television to know about the Kardashians."

I pushed my bowl of pasta away. "You mean that dumb reality television show?"

I'd heard of the Kardashians. Apparently, they live just south of me, in Calabasas.

Fun fact: The city of Calabasas is a landfill for Los Angeles. *And* it's the place where the rich and famous, like Justin Bieber, Jennifer Lopez, Katie Holmes, and many others, have set up camp. The Osbournes originally made it famous with their reality television show. Calabasas is close to Hollywood, but out of the smog and congestion of the city.

Whether you live in Hidden Hills or the Oaks, the exclusive gated properties where many celebrities reside, you're still under scrutiny. It's not enough to live in a neighborhood with ten-million-dollar houses. The residents snub each other based on what gate they live at. They name each other's houses, politely poking fun: The Lemonade Stand, The Ranch, The Crack House. Okay, I might have made up that last one...maybe.

It was a bit ironic to me that the city of Calabasas dumps their garbage in their own backyard, shoving it down year after year, while also working to fund a ten-million-dollar animal crossway. The cougars might have to live among thrown out Prada-purses and empty alkaline water bottles, but they will one day have access to the other side of the 101. Then they can broaden their mating territory and not 'be as incestual as the residents' apparently are. That was told to me by a friend who knows the inner workings of the gated communities and gave me a small peek into the strangeness that goes on there.

The residents of the communities aren't allowed to take out their own garbage because it's seen as crude. Can't have trashcans lining the streets in Hidden Hills. Man, I'm sort of envious, since my neighbors never actually bring their trash cans in from the curb. They just chunk garbage at the open can, hoping that it makes it into the receptacle. When it doesn't, I'm sure they console themselves with the thought that they are composting.

Garbage and landfills aside, this friend told me a quaint story she overheard while at a playdate at a friend's house in one of these gated communities. One of the girls tells my friend's daughter that her grandpa is always shouting at and about his neighbors.

"What does he say?" the other little girl asked.

"Oh, he calls them a bad word and hollers for hours about all the things they do that irritate him."

My friend's daughter leaned forward. "What is the bad word?"

The other little girl cut her eyes at my friend and then whispered, "He calls them a Kardashian. It's always 'damn Kardashian' this and 'damn Kardashian' that."

"What's a Kardashian?" my friend's daughter asked.

The girl shook her head. "I don't know, but it's not good."

The girls played for another hour, and then apparently, my friend's daughter did something the other little girl didn't approve of. So the other little girl grabbed the toy out of her hand and shook her head at her.

"You Kardashian! I don't like it when you do that!"

As I mentioned, Justin Bieber lives in this same gated community. He is the reason I once sat in traffic for three hours, a few miles from my home. The police raided the little jerk's house after some vandalism incident, and the raid locked down the 101, giving me nothing to do but sit in traffic for hours and watch helicopters streak overhead.

My friend Matt works for the property management company who oversees a certain celebrity mansion. Apparently, they pay hundreds of thousands of dollars in fines each year for neighborhood violations. He says they are small things that they could avoid but just pay for in order to not deal with. I can completely relate. I do that all the time with library fines.

Back to lunch. My friend was thoroughly disappointed that I wasn't more excited that we were lunching beside Kendall Jenner. I was disappointed that I was prohibited from speaking for the rest of the meal so that Alissa could eavesdrop. I got to hear all about Kendall's upcoming schedule, which sounded hectic with lots of photo shoots and whatnot.

I'm apparently supposed to care about this kind of stuff, but I live too much in my nerdy world to be impressed by reality television stars. George found it pretty cool that the daughter of a famous rock star was in Eleanor's class. George is in the music industry, so I guess I can appreciate it. I'd much prefer that Eleanor went to school with the daughter of a famous author like Dan Brown or Phillip Pullman.

George was disappointed when I couldn't take Eleanor to this little girl's birthday party.

"Sorry, we already have plans," I said over the phone.

"What are you doing? It can't be cooler than going to a famous rock star's house," he complained.

"We're going to Big Bear," I said. "And I sort of don't

care about hanging out with people just because they're famous."

He sighed, used to my self-righteous bullshit.

Honestly, I might have gotten excited about it if it was one of the obscure folk artists I listen to. But they are all hippies who live in Oregon or Colorado.

I'd like to think that my detachment from Hollywood celebrities makes it easier for the famous people around me to coexist. I always treat them like they're normal because I honestly don't know who they are. I'm fairly certain I've shopped alongside A-list celebrities at Trader Joe's and didn't know it; the big sunglasses and hats were my only clue. However, it is LA, so I know a few divas who are nobodies and wear that get-up just to fool people into thinking they're someone famous. And before you say that A-list celebrities don't do their own grocery shopping, Britney Spears has been seen buying produce many times at the local Albertsons.

LA is a surreal place because the things that shouldn't happen in my ordinary life happen here. I once took my sister to Sky High, a place with a bazillion trampolines lined up in a huge warehouse. It's pretty much the best place in the entire world. My stepmother freaked out when she realized that James Gandolfini was in line in front of us. For a southerner from Baton Rouge, it is not an everyday occurrence to run into a celebrity at a kid's play place; however, this is LA, an actor's playground... therefore, what shouldn't be common has become the norm.

I once sat in Conan O'Brian's desk chair. Go back and tell my younger self that, and she'd laugh in disbelief—I never thought I was getting out of that small East Texas town. And Conan O'Brien wasn't a real person that had a real desk... That was all Hollywood, which is like Mars, full of Martians. But it turns out that Conan is real, and that dude is tall. I had to get a ladder to climb into his chair, which is surprisingly minimalist, about like the simple desk chair I have at home (because I'm cheap).

You're probably wondering about these dinners I have with celebrities. They happen all the time. We don't even plan it. For instance, the other day, I was at my favorite local BBQ restaurant. There's a long set of shared booths, sort of family style. I looked at the table right next to mine and noticed a familiar face: Jerry O'Connell, an actor and husband to Rebecca Romijn. We were both dining with our daughters. We were pretty much at the same table, so by all reasoning, we had dinner together.

On another occasion, I was dining with Eleanor at the Natural Café, and there was no one else at our table. Actually, I had thought we were the only ones at the restaurant, but that was because all my attention was on my child, who was around nine months old at the time. When I used to take Eleanor out to eat, I'd order our food, the check, and a to-go container all at once. You never know if a baby is going to grant you time to eat or throw down the tantrum of the century.

I was trying to cram my veggie burger down my throat as fast as I could when Eleanor became distracted by a couple who had sat down behind us. I didn't look back to see them, only kept chewing as quickly as I could. I'm a little ashamed to admit that I kept my head down as Eleanor twisted around in her seat and began waving incessantly at the people. I knew I should make my daughter turn back around to face the table and not harass strangers, but I also knew that I had half a burger left and limited time to get it down. Finally, when she started babbling, my Southern etiquette kicked in.

I tapped the table to get the baby's attention. "Hey, Elle, let's not bother other people at a restaurant." I then turned to the couple to apologize.

It took me a moment to recognize the faces staring back at me since neither was wearing any makeup. Ellen DeGeneres and Portia de Rossi simply smiled, continuing to wave at my child.

"Don't be silly," Ellen said good-naturedly. "Finish eating, and we'll entertain your baby."

How could I say no to that? I thanked them and spun back around to slowly finish my food, Eleanor busy making faces at the two women.

It was after this experience that I concluded that everyone in LA is an asshole...except for Ellen DeGeneres.

Chapter Fourteen

CAN I HAVE YOUR FRIEND'S NUMBER

I think I'm dating a serial killer, but I'm way too curious to cut him off. We met on Bumble and have been chatting for several months. The guy definitely has a lot of crazy going on, but it's mixed with a charming personality, so I keep him around.

His responses are so wrong, I have to hear what he'll say next. The other day, I told him I was too busy to go out; he wanted to show me around Santa Barbara, where he lives. Only forty minutes from my house, Santa Barbara is a quiet beach town where my blood pressure drops upon entering city limits. The wine flows like wine, and the rich aristocrats mix seamlessly with the hippies, so much so that you can hardly tell them apart.

I informed Serial Killer that I was busy that weekend.

"Too busy for your future husband?" he responded.

I had no answer for that. But you see, that's what I've found so intriguing and wrong about this guy. He doesn't let my silence deter him. Instead, he sends me our astrology compatibility chart. Apparently, according to a bogus source, Virgos and Tauruses are perfect together.

Again, I didn't have a response to that. What was I supposed to say? *This astrology business changed my mind about this weekend. I'll dump Eleanor at her father's house so you can cut me up into little pieces, you psycho?*

That wasn't going to work. Eleanor always comes first. I won't even allow her to go to a friend's house for a slumber party on the weekends I have her. I want all of her time.

"But, Mommy, when am I going to be able to do a sleep-over?" she asked in the whining voice she knows I love.

"When you're thirty," I answered

She sighed. "For real, though. When?"

"Look, it's fine if you want to sleep over at Keeyan's house, but I'm coming too."

My friend Samar, Keeyan's mother, had said it was okay if I tagged along, knowing I didn't want to miss my Elle time.

My little princess then rolled her eyes and stomped her feet. "I want to have a sleepover by myself."

My phone buzzed. I looked at it. Apparently Serial Killer wanted me to have a sleepover all by myself, too. The better to kill me with no witnesses. He had sent me the Carpenters' song, "Close to You," and messaged, "I'm just sitting here plucking these flower petals and thinking of you..."

I was certain he was tearing the petals from an innocent flower and trying to calculate if he had enough chloroform. Again I politely ignored him, which only made him hungrier, it seemed.

The next day, he informed me he was passing through my area.

How convenient.

"Can we do lunch at noon?" he asked. "That's the only time I'm free."

"Oh, too bad, I'm at Pilates."

Five fucking seconds later, he messaged, "Schedule changed. How about one-thirty?"

When I didn't respond immediately, he sent me a GIF from the movie *Titanic* of Leonardo DiCaprio and Kate Winslet embracing. Again, this guy had made me speechless. Not from love, though, but rather from pure amazement.

I knew I needed to cut him loose. Tell him that it wasn't going to work because he was insane and scared me. Too many times, he'd asked to take me out to a secluded beach, where I was certain he planned to drown me like the rest of the women he'd dated. But I just couldn't dump him. I was too curious about what scary things he'd say next.

I think I can look at the men I've dated and see my own mental disorders.

I wasn't ready to cut Serial Killer off, despite all the crazy shit he'd said. It was too entertaining, which plainly meant I'd rather be amused by my dating life than find my soulmate. Somewhere out there, Mr. Right was being slightly normal and not creeping other women out. How very boring. Meanwhile, Serial Killer sent me pictures of myself from my profile and said things like, "I can't look away from these eyes." I interpreted that to mean, 'I want to put them in a box under my bed.'

When I would mention to Serial Killer that we should

do a group date, he'd always shy away from the idea. Then he'd send me a picture of himself at a secluded beach and say, "This is a much better idea for the two of us."

When I went silent, he didn't take the hint, because serial killers don't quit.

"Is it that we live too far apart? I can come to you," he said.

He couldn't come to my house; I know for a fact that my neighbors can't hear me scream, so that wasn't going to work. And before you start thinking something kinky about that statement, just you wait. I'll get to that later.

The distance didn't bother me, to be honest. It was the fact that when I'd casually ask what he was doing, he would always say, "Planning our honeymoon."

I was pretty sure he actually meant my funeral.

Being forty minutes apart was nothing for me. That was a big improvement over my past. One of my last serious relationships, the guy lived on the East Coast. Long-distance relationships are tough unless you're me and independent to a fault. I thrive on long-distance relationships. I get all the electronic attention I need to sustain my fondness for the person, without all the clinginess. Like a pilot, they visit every so often, and best of all, there's no dirty man clogging up my drain with their hair shavings.

Serial Killer not only didn't quit, he never lost confidence—I think that was sort of crucial for his overall mission. As a murderer, the moment doubt enters your mind, you slip up, leave a severed arm behind, and then the police discover the string of murders you've committed.

I, like most girls, prefer confidence. It's probably the most attractive quality that a future mate can portray. I wanted to tell one guy on Bumble that after he messaged me, but I try not to turn into every guy's therapist. I'd be busy forever.

This guy and I matched on Bumble, and I followed the protocol, sending him the first message. Girls making the first move is absolutely against my very nature. My debutant mother actually used to forbid me to call a boy.

"You make them call you," she'd command.

"But what if they don't?" I argued.

"Then it wasn't meant to be."

My mother lived by the philosophy that fate runs our lives. I prefer to take a more hands-on approach these days, but still, it's ingrained in me that guys make the first move. Otherwise I "look like a hussy," "throwing" myself at men.

In my late thirties, I'm working hard to break out of all the programming from my childhood. That's why I put on my best hussy outfit, Daisy Dukes and a halter top, and messaged the guy I'd matched with on Bumble.

A day later, the guy responds with, "you're cute, but I gotta be honest, you're probably out of my league. I'm not even close to having my shit together, and about the only thing I have to bring to the table right now is a good heart. I don't know exactly what you're looking for, just that you can probably do better than me."

Probably? You can't even use proper punctuation, I thought as I read the reply. There was no 'probably' about it.

But why was Mr. Loser even on this dating app if he was going to demoralize himself when a woman reached out to him? I'd never heard such a pathetic reply.

Confidence is key. He could have lived with his parents and played video games all day, but if he'd responded with,

"Hey. You're cute. I've got a lot going on right now, but how about I take you out for a drink when I'm free?" I probably would have said yes. The "a lot going on" might have just been that he was in an online tournament that was super demanding on his schedule. The "when I'm free" part might have been on Tuesday when he'd finally showered.

Yes, I would have eventually figured out that he was a loser and politely ended things, but I might also have fallen for his confidence and given him a real chance. It's hard to tell.

As I said, confidence is key, and definitely something I have to work on, too.

My Pilates instructor-turned-friend Pelé and I have been discussing this dating business. Specifically, how confidence and being bold relate to it. We decided to give each other monthly challenges and hold each other accountable. It's kind of like the buddy system friends use for dieting, except with dating.

"Okay, what's our first challenge?" she asked.

I know that I've become complacent with dating. I won't look a potential man in the eyes in public, and then I string along serial killers online. If I'm being honest, I'm not even trying.

I remembered what my friend Alissa said about getting out of my element, about pushing myself. Then I remembered what my mother told me about never making the first move. *'If they want you, they'll come to you. Play hard to get.'*

That approach, or lack thereof, totally worked for my mother, since she'd been married four times. However, I wasn't concerned with finding a man who wanted to take care of me; I wanted someone who I respected. An equal.

"I think we should have to go up to a man and ask for his number," I said to Pelé.

I couldn't believe the words that had rushed out of my mouth. However, it did make perfect sense. If we were adopting challenges, then this was the perfect one to start with. It forced me to talk to an actual man, in real life. It made it so I had to make the first move. And it definitely meant I had to up my confidence.

"Yes," Pelé agreed. "I'm totally down for that challenge."

Of course, she is, I thought.

Pelé, as my Pilates instructor and a minor pop star, had a lot of things going for her that I didn't. I only mention this because it directly relates to confidence. She's in incredible shape, tall, and has hair and eyelashes that go on for days. I'm like the hobbit form of her.

I was unsurprised that Pelé completed the challenge in the first week.

"You realize we have four weeks to ask for a guy's number," I complained when I found out. "There was no reason to do it right away."

"Why put it off?" she reasoned.

"Because I'm still trying to drop ten pounds," I answered.

She laughed, thinking I was kidding. "It really is a mind trip, though. I never realized what a man has to go through, asking us out."

I thought about it. That was another thing that was stopping me from completing the challenge. The fear of rejection was real. It was painful. I didn't think I could move on with my life if I asked a complete stranger for his phone number and he said no. All of a sudden, I understood the intimidation that men faced when asking me out. Maybe this was why I'd always been overly nice to them, saying yes when I had no interest in dating them. I hoped that the guy I eventually asked for a phone number from would take this pity on me.

"Where did you find this guy you picked up?" I asked.

I was thinking that Pelé would say a bar or a club. Those made the most sense.

I wasn't expecting her to say, "Costco."

"Are you serious?" I asked in disbelief. "What, were you two in line to get samples, and you asked him for his phone number?"

She shrugged. "Sort of. We kept running into each other. After like the tenth time, I decided to talk to him."

"What did you talk about? Moral philosophy? Quantum physics? British literature?"

She grimaced at my question. "I kept it simple. I asked him if he was single."

"Oh," I said, fixing the script I'd been constructing in my head.

I changed it from: ~~"Hi I'm Sarah, a sci-fi writer. I have a daughter and a cat and really like Emily Dickinson's poetry. I'd like to have your phone number if you're amenable."~~ The new script read: "Heya. Are you single?"

"So he gave you his phone number?" I asked, still in disbelief that my friend had picked up a man at Costco. "Are you going to message him?"

"We already have lunch set up for tomorrow," she reported.

Damn. I had a lot to learn from Pelé. Getting the

number was just the first part of the challenge. Then I'd have to follow up.

"Sarah, it's really hard to do, but once you do it, you'll have a whole new confidence," Pelé said.

The next day, I couldn't wait to hear how the date with Costco Guy went.

"Well?" I asked Pelé during class.

"It was fun," she responded. "He's nice."

"And cute?" I inquired.

She nodded. "Yeah, I got a picture of him." She pulled up her phone and scrolled through until she found Costco Guy. "See?"

My mouth popped open at the sight of the man on her phone. "That guy has kids at my daughter's school. I see him at drop-off every day," I told her.

"Oh my God!" Pelé exclaimed.

"And now you see why I can't pick up a guy at Costco," I stated.

She agreed with a nod. "Your situation is a bit more complex. You and I are going to the club this weekend."

When Saturday night came, I tried to make excuses for why I couldn't go.

"I have to work," I said to Pelé.

"This *is* work," she countered. "Aren't you writing a book about dating in LA?"

Damn her and her excellent reasoning.

"I haven't lost those ten pounds yet," I continued.

I think I was actually up three pounds, but who was counting.

"You're fine," she stated. "And it's only a phone number

you have to get, not the rest of your life. Besides, you have salon hair."

That was the best point she could have made. I had gone to the salon that morning. Having a stylist do one's hair is the fastest way to up confidence. Somehow, my stylist has a way of doing my hair that makes me suddenly look younger, thinner and more radiant. It's like she's my fairy godmother, waving a magic wand and transforming me for the night. However, it lasts way past midnight. If I don't wash my hair, it lasts for several days. Thank the gods for dry shampoo, am I right ladies?

Unable to argue with Pelé, I agreed to go.

We got to the club at around eleven, which was pretty much two hours after my bedtime.

"If you don't stop yawning, I'll make your ass pay," she said as we parked.

I knew that her threat was serious. She would make me do so many butt crunches the next week, I'd cry for mercy. I'm a grown adult who can do as I like, unless I'm paying gobs of dollars to have someone make me work out—then I do whatever they say. Otherwise, it just seems like a waste of money, and we all know how frugal I am.

We breezed by the bouncer, who recognized Pelé. Once in the club, the DJ also recognized her, shouting out from the microphone.

"You're sort of a celebrity," I admired.

"I've performed here," she stated casually.

"I have, too."

"You have?" she asked with disbelief.

"Well, yeah, until they kicked me off the stage," I said, pointing to where the DJ was.

Tequila had been involved that night, which, as we've discussed, is never a good idea for me. I hadn't really been kicked off the stage, so much as the club was shutting down. However, while on tequila, I have no concept of time. I remember going to the bathroom, and when I came out, the club was empty.

I shook my head at the bouncer beside the stage, unaware at the time that the DJ was packing up his equipment. "Man, this place really isn't doing so hot," I said to him, knowing he was also the manager of the club. "I've got a Master's in business if you want some pointers on how to improve things here."

The guy gave me a good-humored smile. "Sure thing, but your Uber is here."

"Wait," I said in disbelief. "But it's not supposed to be here until after two in the morning." My friends and I had made arrangements ahead of time, the gang wanting to stay out as late as possible.

"That's right, sweetheart." He pointed to the exit. "The girls are all waiting for you out there since we've shut down the club."

I gulped, realizing that tequila and I never needed to spend time together. It would only end with me marching across the desert in Las Vegas, firmly believing that not sleeping for thirty-six hours was totally fine.

After Pelé scored us a round of free drinks from the bartender, who, unsurprisingly, knew her, it was time for me to make my move.

"Just pick someone and start talking to them," she encouraged. "Everyone here is single. That's why they are here."

I nodded, gathering my confidence, which was about like trying to pick up sand with a net.

"That guy looks cute," I said, pointing to a man with dark hair and a nice smile. More importantly, he wasn't surrounded by a horde of his friends.

Pelé pushed me, which I sort of found abusive, but I wasn't going to mention it, since she's taller and so much stronger than me.

"Hey, there," I said to the guy at the bar, trying to remember my script.

I hadn't gotten out the next line before he shook his head at me.

"Sorry, I just got out of a relationship," he yelled over the loud music.

And right then, my confidence plummeted. However, I plastered a fake smile on my face.

"Uhhh...I was just going to ask if you'd hand me a napkin," I said, pointing behind his back where a stack of cocktail napkins sat.

"Oh, right," the guy said, looking embarrassed. "Sorry. Of course."

He turned around and grabbed a napkin, thrusting it into my hand, the one not holding the perspiring wine glass.

"Thanks," I said and turned around, muttering under my breath, "you dumb asshole."

Who goes to a club right out of a relationship? Then I reminded myself, *Every guy ever.* And besides, he may have just been making that up. I'm not everyone's type; I'm short, have a resting bitch face that keeps most at bay, and a conservative dress code.

When I rejoined Pelé, she was surrounded by three

guys. *Shocking.* Before she could ask how it went, I shook my head roughly. She seemed to understand my nonverbal communication.

"This is my new friend Nick. He was just about to show me pictures of his cat," Pelé said loudly, indicating the guy next to her. "Don't you have a cat, Sarah?"

"Yeah," I said, defeat heavy in my voice. I snapped my fingers at the guy next to Pelé. "Let's see your cat photos."

The guy was sort of handsome, but a bit too young for me. Actually, he was way too young for me; he was never going to get any of my 1980s references. However, I reminded myself this was about confidence, not about finding the man of my dreams.

Baby steps, I told myself.

"A fellow cat lover," the guy said, winking at me. "Pelé tells me she's allergic, which is too bad."

"Yeah, she'll never know the joy of waking up to find a cat purring on her chest, looking down at her with a deranged stalker smile," I said.

The guy laughed. "Said like a true cat owner." He pulled up a photo on his phone and handed it to me. "That's my best friend, Pluto."

I took one look at his phone and shrank away in disgust. "Dude, that's fucking animal abuse. How heavy is your cat?"

And there was that look of offense I was so good at producing on other people's faces. I hadn't even had any tequila...yet.

"He's roughly twenty pounds."

I shook my head. "Do you shove food down his throat?"

He laughed uncomfortably. "Pluto has a thyroid problem."

I clapped my hand to my chest. "So do I!"

Maybe everything was going to work out for the best after all. I hadn't lost those ten pounds, but maybe Nick wouldn't care.

He nodded. "I have to give him medicine, but he's my best friend, so I don't mind. Whatever it takes."

"I'm sorry that I called your cat fat and insinuated you're a bad cat dad."

"That's okay," he said. "I'm guessing your cat isn't fat, then?"

I shook my head. "No, Finley, my cat, takes Pilates with me. Pelé keeps his ass in shape," I joked.

The guy laughed, cutting his eyes at Pelé, who was enjoying the attention of the other two guys.

"Yeah, it's tough to ensure they get enough exercise," Nick said. "I've been struggling with it."

This might have been my perfect scenario. I was talking to a man about *his cat*. The universe had given me the perfect setup.

"Hey, why don't you give me your number, and we can exchange ways to keep our cats healthy?" I suggested, instantly wondering if this strange approach would work. All I had to do was get the phone number.

He didn't throw his drink in my face, as I expected. He didn't shrink back and say he was in a committed relationship with his cat or that he'd just gotten out of a relationship.

"Sure thing," Nick said.

And right then, I had done it. I'd completed my first mission. Victory was sweet and it filled up the confidence meter, ensuring more future successes. Nick might be too young for me, based on my standards, but he'd agreed to give me his phone number.

"You realize you still have to text him," Pelé said as she drove me home that night...well, early morning.

"Even though there's no potential of a future?" I asked.

She nodded. "It's about strengthening your dating muscle."

I agreed with her as I got out of her car.

The next morning, I crafted the perfect, casual message to Nick: "Hey, how is Pluto? Tell him Finley says 'hi.'"

I nervously waited a couple of minutes, as the dots popped up, indicating that Nick was messaging me back.

"Hey! He's good, and we're both looking forward to hearing those fitness tips."

I was just about to send him a picture of this new toy I'd gotten for Finley and that he loved when another message came through.

"Hey, is your friend single? The taller, blonder one?"

I wasn't sure why he was describing Pelé. It wasn't like I needed to be reminded that she was the hotter friend.

"Yeah, she totally is," I messaged back.

"Cool, can I have her number?"

I'm a good friend; that's why I deleted Nick. There was no future for him and Pelé. Not only because he abused his cat by overfeeding it, but also because he had a shitty memory and didn't recall that she was allergic to cats.

Chapter Fifteen

MY YOGA INSTRUCTOR TOUCHED MY ASS

Yoga is my church. When I first divorced and moved back to Southern California, I knew I had to renovate myself. I actually had a fair amount of anxiety. Newly divorced, with a five-year-old depending on me, trying to pay the high cost of LA living and sticking all my time and money into my books. Go figure that I was stressed.

My friends kept urging me to date or go out with them, but I didn't have a spare moment. Then one day, while Eleanor and I were making mud cakes in the backyard, a full-on panic attack hit me. I couldn't understand it. I had taken my life back. I had a beautiful home. I was playing on a Wednesday afternoon with my daughter because my schedule afforded such a luxury, and yet, my body was telling me I was not okay.

The body never lies. It knows that which the mind is trying to suppress.

I realized then that I had to start therapy and figure out some coping techniques. I really wanted to talk about

George, explain to a nonbiased person why the relationship didn't work. Let the guilt of divorcing him roll out of me.

But that's not what happened.

I chose a cognitive behavioral therapist, who focused on offering tools rather than listening to problems. I did learn things that helped me immensely. For instance, when panic set in, I immediately asked myself, "Is this real, am I in danger?" and then I'd try to breathe into the space in my body that was closing up. It was from doing this technique that I learned there was no extra space in my body. It was all congested with emotions and frustrations. Regrets. Things I'd allowed to go unsaid.

I don't believe in allowing fate to rule my life. However, I do believe that if I put something out into the universe, it will conspire to offer me that which I seek. I have to be willing to say yes, though.

I was managing with my stress, when one day, a Groupon happened to catch my attention. In LA, Groupons are how we check out most things, from paddle boarding to sushi. Why pay full price when we can get a deal and try something out?

I purchased a Groupon for what I thought was yoga classes but got an invaluable deal for something way more than some stretching and deep breathing.

I entered that small studio a bundle of stress, not having taken a proper breath in two or three years. The instructor, a calm hippie from Topanga Canyon with a European accent, said something that first day that has stuck with me ever since.

"Wherever you are today is where you're supposed to be."

It struck me in the chest. I'd been holding onto so much guilt since the divorce, punishing myself constantly for not being able to make things work with George. However, as I looked around from where I was perched on my foam yoga mat, I realized I was exactly where I needed to be in life.

Every time I looked backward, I was in jeopardy of going back that way. And every time I looked forward, I clenched my eyes shut, so afraid of where I was headed.

The instructor, Sami, who has become my spiritual guide, started telling me something every week that chipped away at the concrete that had formed in my body, creating stiffness.

"I'm only helping you to connect with your own inner wisdom," she explained to me one day when I told her she couldn't take a day off to teach senior citizens yoga.

"But, Sami, I need your help," I said, realizing I was whining slightly. "Since I've been coming to your class, I've found space in my body. The other instructors aren't as good as you."

Sami's good nature prevented her from saying anything about my jab. She simply smiled, probably dialing up Buddha in her head for a proper reply.

"That one instructor played Elvis and live concert music the entire time," I continued to complain. "I left class more stressed than when I started."

"I understand, Amber," Sami said.

Side note: I've been taking a class from Sami for years now, and she still calls me Amber. I've let it go on for so long that I can't bring myself to correct her at this point. She'd be mortified, and the last thing I'd do is make my guru so upset, she may potentially not guide my practice.

"Yoga is about finding peace within ourselves," Sami continued. "And when we find that in ourselves, we find it for others. Then the things that bothered us before aren't as big of a deal."

Sami had repeatedly tried to drill this "namaste" crap into me. I got the concept: 'the light within me honors the light within you.' I totally understood it, except when dumbasses pissed me off in traffic.

I like hippie bullshit, which is why I feel at home on the West Coast. However, it's important to note that, although I drive a Prius and rarely brush my hair, I'm not a dirty hippie. When I lived in Oregon, I strangely found the hippies to be the most judgmental types. They were the ones who gave me disapproving looks for using sunscreen or plastic bags.

Needless to say, I got a little fed up with hippies when I confined myself to Ashland, Oregon for two years. I nearly plowed over the entire Birkenstock-wearing population to get out of there. I can't live in a town where naked children with dreadlocks crawl around on the co-op floor, while the store manager plays a ukulele in the parking lot.

Because of these experiences, my tolerance for hippies is low. However, not only can I stand Sami, I fucking love the woman. When she talks about equinox shit, I don't want to murder her.

"Today, to honor the autumn equinox, I invite you to recognize the cosmic equinity through breath exercises," Sami said one day.

I was only hoping that meant we got to lie in pigeon pose for ten minutes. The hips, in yoga, are considered the emotional junk drawer of the body, and mine are always overflowing with shit I don't need.

Sami guided us through the poses, having us hold triangle—another of my favorite poses—a little longer than usual. She's a hands-on instructor, which took me by surprise the first time she touched my butt in an attempt to fix my alignment.

I looked at her and said, "You haven't even bought me a drink yet."

That was my first class with her, and ever since then, she's been trying to get me to loosen up and be more accepting. She may not cast a judgmental look at me, but I know she sees when I'm obsessing over my hair instead of dropping down into warrior one. I'm also aware that Sami sees the scowls I give to the other students in class. In my defense, it's because they are a bunch of undisciplined fuckers who need to learn some manners.

I'm such an asshole that I glare with disdain at the late arrivals in yoga class. And don't even get me started on those who fucking crowd my mat. I always shoot them murderous looks. I was in class the other day, and you'd think I was fucking Beyoncé, by how much everyone wanted up on my junk. There was loads of space all over the room, but everyone kept throwing down their mats inches from mine, totally boxing me in.

Namaste to all, except that fucker whose feet I had to look at, inches from my face, when in upward dog. And to the blonde grandma whose ass I was staring at from close range, I don't appreciate that the light within you is the light within me. Oh, and you're eighty. How in the hell is your hair so blonde?

Then there was the woman who barged into yoga class ten minutes late. Buddha doesn't like her because she broke my focus. I don't care that she just got out of spin class; leave that class early to get to yoga on time! This is my fucking church. Would you come to mass late, throwing your purse down loudly while I'm praying to Jesus? No, I didn't think so. Respect my religion, or whatever this is for me. It might not be saving my soul, but it's keeping me from killing you, which is important for both of us.

And how are ninety percent of the people in my yoga class blonde? That defies the odds of the population. Blonde hair color is a recessive gene, which means it's impossible that four out of every five women in the class are light-haired. Well, I'm a blonde—just look at Eleanor. There's my proof. I gave her that beautiful golden hair. And although I don't have blonde hair anymore, I have to keep it up to match her. But ninety percent of the class wasn't born blonde, let's be honest.

I'm all too aware that my superficial judgments are blocking my chi. I'm fucking working on it.

"Your only concern is what happens on your mat," Sami encouraged, probably provoked by the angry stare I was giving the redhead who kept checking out her butt in the mirror.

She was wearing a short top that showed off her abs. Okay, it was a sports bra. And her ass cheeks were hanging out of her shorts, which would have been tiny even on my daughter. After watching her turn around several times to eye her ass, I shot her a disapproving look, which Sami caught. I felt like I was in elementary school again, and the teacher was about to scold me.

Instead, Sami said, "When we find something in yoga that challenges us, it's better to breathe through it than run from it or bottle it up."

So I can't punch the redheaded bimbo in the face, then?

"Amber, I invite you to tuck in your naval and your pelvic floor," Sami said, and I realized a moment later she was talking to me.

I'm Amber! Right.

I never thought that cobra pose was going to liberate me from my asshole tendencies, but I've worked hard to try and create that stillness in my body.

"It's not about achieving the pose, it's about being able to breathe," Sami said, her sage witness reminding me yet again that I was holding my breath.

Then she fucked everything up.

"For the rest of the month, I won't be here. I'm going to a yoga retreat on an island in Newfoundland."

Dammit, motherfucker!

Was it too much to ask that my yoga instructor teach me regularly? I only got to take classes on the weekends I didn't have Eleanor, and that was barely enough to keep my anger management problems in check.

The last time Sami had a substitute, the freak brought in a sound bath. The hippie explained that the noise the crystal bowl made when rubbed was "washing the soul."

Man, I have heard some hippie-ass-shit in my time, but that had to take the vegan cake.

"The sound bath awakens your inner guide while putting the ego to sleep," the dumb substitute said as we all lay in savasana, also known as corpse pose.

"I invite you all to open yourself up for this concert of

the soul," the instructor said, making a deep humming sound with the bowl.

I was starting to feel like a popular sorority girl, I was being invited to so many things in yoga.

I did have to admit that there was a calming aspect to the sound bath, but that might have only been because it drowned out the bass shaking the walls from the spin class.

When we rose from our meditation, my soul wasn't singing the tunes it had heard, but I might have felt a little more tolerant of the people crowded around me, even if they weren't real blondes. No one in LA really is... well, except for me. And Ellen DeGeneres.

Still sleepy-eyed from nearly falling asleep during the meditation, I blinked at the instructor, a hippie who probably hadn't changed her clothes in a fortnight. She probably wouldn't until the next equinox. That's how you achieve balance, right?

She'd come around to offer us gentle massages during the meditation portion of the class, which I was much more receptive to since Sami had started touching my butt all the time.

"Thank you," I said from a seated position, my hands in front of my chest. "Namaste."

"Namaste," she said, bowing her head to me.

I decided then that Sami might not be the only hippie I like. This girl had helped me to create space in my body. And when I wanted to flee from the room, challenged by the pose, her words came at the right time.

"Remember that bringing your mind back to the present moment is where the magic happens," the substitute said.

"That was actually a good class," I said, rolling up my

mat and quietly punishing myself for saying the word 'actually.'

"I'm glad you enjoyed it," the hippie said, not picking up on my slip. She eyed me a bit cautiously. "What did you dream about last night?"

For a moment, I was utterly thrown off by the question. There couldn't be anything more random than this sudden inquiry about my sleep last night.

"I don't know," I answered truthfully.

This earned me a disappointed look from the woman, like I should have recorded all my dreams in my journal next to my bed upon waking.

"How about you?" I said, trying to be nice.

"Oh, I dreamed I was swimming with the dolphins," she said. "I was going to take pictures of them and then decided to live in the moment. When I woke up, I researched the meaning in my books and learned that it meant that not just my mind was open, but my other mind."

"Uhhh...okay."

Damn, fucking hippies never made any sense. They always made feel high when I talked to them.

Chapter Sixteen

MY NEIGHBORS CAN'T HEAR ME SCREAM

Because I own a cat, approximately twenty percent of men automatically disqualify me on the dating app. Apparently, loving an animal that is distant and stingy with its affection reflects on my character. I think that getting a dog would normalize this effect, but I haven't figured out which one of my friends' Labradoodles I'm stealing yet. And I'd have to dye the dog's fur, so my friend doesn't recognize that it's their animal when we're at the park.

With a sad face, one of the old guys will say, "That dog looks a lot like Cocoa."

Because I'll not have completed the training to desensitize the animal to its old name, it might look up at its old owner.

"Yeah, well this dog is pink, not cocoa-colored. Besides, its name is Zuma because I named it after a famous literary character."

"Oh, what book is the character Zuma from?" the guy will ask.

I'll gawk at him in offense. "It's from one of mine, duh."

When I got the cat for Eleanor, I told her that he had to be named after a literary character.

"That's the rule," I stated firmly.

"But I wanted to name him 'Twilight Sparkle' or 'Princess Celestia'," she said, referencing My Little Pony.

I shook my head. "Those are mouthfuls, and he's no princess," I said, looking down at the black and white kitten who only weighed two pounds. I'd gotten him from the animal shelter, unlike my asshole neighbors who got their dogs from breeders. Hadn't they listened to Bob Barker? Spay and neuter your pet to control the pet population, don't breed a bunch of animals so that mutts congest the animal shelters.

"I always name my animals after literary characters," I explained to Eleanor. "I've had Gatsby, Huxley, and Ginny. This little guy will be named after a famous character like Harry or Finley."

"I know that Harry is from Harry Potter," Eleanor began, "but where does Finley come from?"

I gawked at my child in offense. "Have you not read *any* of my books?"

She shook her head. "I'm only five years old."

I rolled my eyes. Readers always had excuses. "Finley is an acrobat in one of my series."

The kitten, who'd only cost me five dollars—not three thousand—jumped out of Eleanor's arms and climbed up my drapes.

I raced over, yelling as he clawed up the once pristine fabric.

There was also a real safety issue with him being on the

drapes. When we'd moved into the townhouse, I'd hung those drapes myself. Not having to do any handiwork for the twelve years before, my toolbox skills were seriously rusty. I literally ended up nailing the drapes into the wall after stripping a dozen screws. It's not safe to even stand under the ones on the northern side of the house; they will stay in the house when I leave because they can't come down.

After encouraging the little fucker down, I handed him back to Eleanor. "Take your cat and teach him some manners."

She smiled at the little guy and said, "I think he's an acrobat. I'm naming him Finley."

I was about to smile with pride when little Finley sneezed on my child. Later I would realize that five-dollar kittens adopted from the animal shelter actually cost five hundred dollars, after all the vet bills are paid.

Finley has since grown up to be a fine member of the household. He is a lovely companion to Eleanor, following her around dutifully. I can often find him lounging beside her while she plays with Legos in her room—a set of toys I desperately wanted when I was little. I also dearly wanted to play with my brother's Transformers and Hot Wheels, but he would have punched me if I ever touched them. Instead, I was given non-engineering toys like Barbies and baby dolls.

And that's why I can't do math. Thanks, Mom.

Finley growing up with Eleanor has worked out great. He's protective of her, constantly watching over her every move. He also thinks I can't feed her properly, which is quite astute since everyone knows I can't cook. I usually just slice up cheese and veggies and throw them on the dinner table. I think I've gone more than six months without using the stove. Not the microwave, though, mind you. I'm not a fucking hippie who is scared of the radiation that thing gives off. It heats up my tea, and sipping on green tea is the only humane part of most days.

Because Finley must suspect that I'm horrible at providing a balanced diet for my daughter, he delivers a mostly dead lizard to her almost every day. He has a cat door that I should board up, but I'm too lazy to be a doorman and frisk him upon entry. So because I'm lazy and an inept cook, he likes to leave these tailless lizards under her seat at the dining table.

I think when I start screaming, "For fuck's sake, not again!" Finley thinks I'm praising him in Catonese for bringing in another bloody lizard. I'm not.

I then hurry off to grab the broom and dustpan, also known as the "mostly-dead animal removal device." Hurrying over to the lizard, who is playing possum, I get it trapped and take it outside, where I chuck it into my neighbor's yard. I reason that they won't notice the dead lizard, with all the beer cans and flea market finds littering their patio.

What's most surprising about my little hunter is that he is confined to a small patio and still manages to bring in quite a few pests. And he won't leave the patio, even though he can climb the various fruit trees.

"How do you manage to make the cat mind?" my nice, civilized neighbor asked me one day when I was hanging from the orange tree, picking the fruit.

"I told him not to, and since then, he knows not to climb the tree," I stated.

"But he keeps bringing in lizards?"

"I haven't figured out the right translation for that message," I admitted, my legs kicking as I struggled to reach a plump orange.

"Do you think that's safe?" my neighbor asked from the ground, pointing at me.

I looked down at where Eleanor was standing under me with a basket. "Probably not. Elle, back up in case I fall. I don't want to hit you."

In an unfortunate incident, I'd lost Ginny, my last cat to coyotes. My neighbor had experienced the same tragedy with his cat. Coyotes own the night in this part of LA, waking me up at all hours with their yipping.

However, if any cat was going to give a coyote a good run, it would be Finley. He's a hunter, and more agile than even the spriteliest cat, catching only the animals who cross into his territory.

On Easter morning, I came down to hear a scurrying I associate with trouble.

I paused on the stairs. "What the fuck are you doing, cat?"

Finley's head perked up from the ottoman. Under it, I saw something furry.

"Oh, fuck." I sighed, going off to collect the dustpan and broom.

Rubbing her eyes, Eleanor came down the stairs behind me. "What is it, Mommy?"

I looked under the ottoman, letting out a breath of relief. "Thank the gods it's not another mouse."

"Is it a bird again?" she asked.

I reached under the ottoman, shooing the cat away. I pulled out a small, fluffy bunny. "No, for a first, it's something I don't mind touching."

Eleanor rushed forward, her eyes wide with excitement, having woken up instantly from the sight of the bunny. "Can I hold it?"

I didn't think the thing had fleas or teeth that would tear into her. I shrugged and handed her the bunny.

"Why don't you release him," I suggested, opening the back door. "I bet his bunny family is worried about him."

Eleanor carried the bunny over to the door carefully and gingerly let him down. Probably not believing that his freedom was real, the bunny remained quite still for several moments before springing off. It was only then that I realized that we'd released the fucking Easter bunny!

Dammit to hell! I didn't even make my wish!

Finley probably gets pretty pissed that we release all of his hard-earned catches, but I couldn't care less. The cat runs enough of the house. I've lost my patience when it comes to pests living in my house. I'm not absolutely certain that I've even caught all of the lizards he's brought into the house, and I fear there might be a family of tailless lizards under the couch.

Because Finley doesn't know his true place in the household, he screams at me while I'm in the shower. Eleanor and I like to joke that he's telling me to get out so he can get ready for work. In our make-believe world, he takes the bus to his accounting firm, where he crunches numbers and bores colleagues with his boring work stories.

Again, accountants, no one wants to hear about the silly accounting error you found. Ever.

When I've gotten tired of the cat harassing me, and make my way out of the shower, I have to be careful to hold onto the railing, because Finley will trip me trying to get into the dripping stall as I open the door. He doesn't wait for me to get all the way out before he's rolling around on the wet surface of the tub.

Even though I give the cat fresh water every day, he prefers the soapy stuff on the bottom of the tub, licking it up quickly before it dries. Once he's completely drenched, he goes outside to roll in the dust. Then it's off to sleep on the white comforter on my bed for the rest of the day.

And that's why I can't have anything nice. Fucking cat!

In the summer, I was sleeping downstairs because I'm too cheap to air-condition the upper story. Eleanor was at George's, which meant that I'd fallen asleep on the sofa after staying up too late watching New Girl.

Side note: my friend, Anne, acts just like Jess from the show, which means that I can't look at her without laughing.

Anyway, I woke up to a squeaky noise, like a dog was chewing on a toy. Finley made the familiar scurrying noise.

I bolted upright. "What the fuck, cat?"

Behind the entertainment center, I could just make out a hairy form. I approached with great caution, my eyes trying to focus. I told myself that what he'd brought in this time was a mouse. A giant fucking mouse. However, once I got up close and saw the long, thick tail curled around the thing, I had to admit to myself that it was, in fact, a rat. A large one.

"Get it, Finley!" I yelled at the cat.

Interesting note: when a cat chomps on a rat, or the rodent is hit with a broom, it makes that squeaky noise like a dog's toy. Apparently, that's where the noise came from. Art imitates life, so there you go.

I decided to open up the house and turn on all the lights, not really knowing what to do.

Finley dutifully went after the rat as I went to fetch the broom and dustpan. However, I realized I had a big fucking problem: I couldn't scoop up the ten-pound rat like I did with the other pests. Firstly, he wasn't going to fit. Secondly, I didn't want to get bit and get the plague.

The rat came out from behind the entertainment center, winding around the furniture. I don't endorse animal abuse, but again, I also don't like the plague. So I slammed the broom down on the vermin. It made that loud squeaky noise, but, undeterred, kept running for the drapes by the dining room. The ones that were precariously hanging, ready to come down with the slightest tug. The rat latched onto the drapes, about to streak up them.

Fuck, I can never have anything nice. I just knew the fucker was going to tear my drapes to hell, just like the asshole-cat who had brought him into the house in the beginning.

At this point, Finley was utterly tuckered out. He decided it was time to retire upstairs for a nap.

"Finley! Don't you leave me down here with this thing!" I yelled, not even thinking that I could be waking up my neighbors. The asshole neighbors on one side of me had woken me up enough times. It was payback.

I ran after the cat, carrying him back downstairs, and positioning him as close to the rat as I dared to get. Keep in mind that I was half-asleep and didn't really understand my options. That's why when Finley turned his nose up at the rat, who was fucking playing dead, and left again, I sat down on the couch and put my head between my knees. I started going through my options. *Do I call the fire department to get the rat out of the house? Do I set fire to the house first and **then** call the fire department?* I didn't know how to handle this, but I was moments away from moving out of my place, leaving everything to the rat.

Feeling like I was out of options, I looked up just as the rat streaked through the house. I screamed clear and loud, my best scream. The one I would have given if an axe murderer had entered my house.

The rat, I realize now, wanted nothing to do with me. He hightailed it for the open door, realizing this was his chance to get away from the vicious cat. He leapt through the door and darted out past the fence.

The next day, still trying to recover from the trauma, I went to my "good" neighbor's house to apologize.

"I'm sorry if my screaming woke you guys up last night," I said to my neighbor, explaining what happened.

He consoled me and then shook his head. "I can understand fearing what Finley will bring in next. However, more concerning to me is that we can't hear if you're screaming."

I made a mental note that I needed to get a dog sooner rather than later. As a bonus, with a dog in my profile picture, I'd appear less bitchy, and more guys would swipe right on me on the dating app.

Chapter Seventeen

I'M LIKE A NINE-YEAR-OLD BOY

Dating is fucking time-consuming. Just to match with a guy on the dating app takes hours, it seems. Weeding through the profiles is work. And unlike what I hear men on the site do, I comb through the bios and photos meticulously. If there is a urinal in one of your photos, it's a hard no. If you're throwing gang signs, I swipe left. If you have more than one photo with your mom, I'm going to pass. My friend Alissa tells me that men have told her that they swipe right on every girl just because they know that, on Bumble, the girl makes the first move. When I painstakingly craft a response to this guy I've matched with, he hasn't even reviewed my profile yet. He's using that first communication to qualify me, and that's just wrong.

I took a break from dating for the summer just because I didn't have a few extra hours each day to swipe. Once I do match with a guy, ninety percent of them turn into my pen pals. When I was ten, I had a pen pal from France named

Pepe. Guess what I don't need in my life currently? If you guessed another Pepe, you're correct.

I usually prefer to meet up with a guy soon after matching to see right away if there is any chemistry. That's actually less time-consuming than sending long messages back and forth with a dozen guys. However, I was recently reminded of the importance of those initial interactions on chat. Some red flags can be raised in the very beginning.

For instance, I was messaging with this really pleasant guy. Yes, there was a bong store behind him in one of his photos, and in another, he was in the back of a truck with a slew of kids. My first thought was that it was highly illegal to drive with children in a flatbed, although that's how I got pretty much everywhere growing up. We didn't have these booster seats back in my day. Hell, I was usually hanging out of the station wagon window, trying to get away from my mother's cigarette smoke.

Anyway, I told myself that I was being too uptight per usual, and needed to give this nice guy a shot. I messaged him, and through our initial interactions, I learned that he was one of fourteen children.

"Wait, what?" I messaged him. "You mean step-siblings, right?"

"No, it's actually eighteen if you count my step sisters and brothers," he replied.

I don't mean to judge, but holy fuck! Overbreeding is a serious issue that I thought I got away from when I moved out of Texas. My sister has six children. When she used to bug me about having children, I'd tell her that she'd hit the quota for the both of us. I was *not* putting out babies to counteract what she'd done.

I'm sorry if this makes me an asshole, but I can't date a guy who has seventeen siblings. I just had a panic attack *thinking* about the holidays. We'd no doubt be crammed into a double-wide trailer with a zoo of people who had all overbred, because the habit is actually hereditary.

As proof of that, the guy, it turns out, at the age of thirty-eight has three children. Two of those kids are in college, which totally blew my mind. Breeding is a learned behavior, and this guy had obviously learned that clogging up our systems with too many unwanted children was okay. To his credit, he spoke fondly of his mother, who birthed these fourteen children. She obviously hated free time and money.

Anyway, I totally went silent on the guy after this conversation. However, through those initial messages, I dodged a bullet that would have been fatal if I had gone out on a date with the guy. There's no way I would have kept a straight face when he told me he was one of fourteen children. I would have offended him, and then his clan of a family would have it out for me.

Usually, I'm the one who says the stuff that pushes the guys away. I can say that confidently because of the many, many men who have ghosted me after I've said something. There was this one guy who was always scuba diving and traveling to Indonesia, Japan, and other exotic places. A real overachiever. Men who travel all the time and have expensive hobbies like surfing and golfing intimidate the fuck out of me. Also, side note, looking at a surfer's abs makes me instantly want to do laundry. *Bring that washboard over here, momma needs to wash up.*

Anyway, this guy and I were chatting over text, and he

said that he thought it was cool that I'm into space opera, and that it's rare to find a female science fiction writer. I couldn't just accept the compliment and be happy that a man found this aspect of my character attractive; no, I had to say, "Yeah, well, I love spaceships and blowing shit up. Deep down inside, I'm a nine-year-old boy."

And he never responded after that.

That was fine because I didn't know how to respond to his stories about backpacking across Europe or skydiving over the Andes on the weekend.

"That's cool," I'd responded. "This weekend, Elle and I got takeout and watched Mama Mia. Afterward, I had to explain to her about premarital sex. It was interesting. She totally didn't think Meryl Streep's character was a slut."

I think I also offended this hot Asian guy. And before you say it, I don't know why I had to mention that he was Asian. It's just part of the context. Oh, and I'm off Asians until after Halloween, remember. However, this guy's shirtless photo sort of earned him a swipe right. Also, I really had a great opening line, or at least I thought so. In the shirtless photo, he was holding an axe. Therefore, I couldn't resist, and messaged him and said, "Hey, nice abs. You're not an axe murderer, though, are you?"

I didn't realize at the time that I'd objectified him while also insinuating that he was a crazy murderer. He never responded, so I think I overstepped some boundaries. I'm sorry, not sorry.

Since dating is so time-consuming, but not something I can keep putting off, I've figured out a system. On the weekend, Eleanor and I have slumber parties, curling up and watching Disney movies. Side note, yet again: I never watched the classic Disney movies. There was no Little Mermaid, 101 Dalmatians or Beauty and the Beast on my television. I grew up with older siblings, and my mother hated cartoons. This meant that if I wanted to watch TV, I had to settle for Law and Order or MASH. And my siblings, who were bigger and meaner than me, always got to pick out the movie rentals. Because of that, I watched Silence of the Lambs at age eight. I haven't slept properly since.

Anyway, due to the neglect of my childhood, I've been trying to catch up on all the Disney movies I've never seen. While Elle and I are watching the Little Mermaid, I spend that time swiping. It's what I do best: multi-tasking.

It's getting easier to weed through the profiles, and I enjoy doing it while watching movies that disempower women. I'm sort of glad I didn't watch the princess movies growing up; I might not have become a science fiction writer if gender roles had been engrained in me early on.

I know I discussed dating profile dos and don'ts before, but there are some reasons I need to revisit these lists. For one, there are literally so many things I see wrong with these profiles. Seriously, men, if you can't present yourself in a way that doesn't make me want to throw up, I'm not sure there's much hope.

For instance, if I read another profile where a man lists sex as one of his hobbies, I'm going to scream. Oh, and fuck the guy who says, "Good sex." And no, I don't mean that literally—that's what he wants. But the idiot thought that clarifying that he was into good sex was at all necessary... As opposed to bad sex? But that's what I'm into. Sorry, it's not going to work because of *that*.

Almost as worse are the men (and there are many) who

state they like eating food. What the fuck? That's like putting breathing on your profile. Can we stop putting obvious shit on our profiles?

Hey, I'm a woman from Earth. I breathe, eat and sleep. Looking for a man who is alive. I like to exist. If that sounds like you, swipe right.

And because LA is full of people who want me to kill them, there's a ton of men who also put that they enjoy eating good food. Again, this isn't necessary, but you're not smart enough for me to even point this out. You should meet this dipshit who likes good sex.

Then there are the fuckers who state they like to have fun. "I like to smile and have a good time." Oh wow, I'm glad you made that disclaimer up front. I fucking hate smiling. And a good time, no thank you. I'm going to swipe left while I eat my awful food and look for a guy with a micropenis.

As you can tell, I could go on and on about how guys put the most obvious shit on their profiles. It has become such a problem, that I literally have nothing to go off of when sending my first communication to them.

"Hey, Mr. Person. This is crazy, but if you can believe it, I like to be happy too! What are the odds? I think you're my soulmate."

Moving on. If any of your profile pictures look like mug shots, it's a hard no. If you're sipping on wine in your picture, I will probably swipe right, thinking that I get some of that wine. I will admit that I swiped right on a guy who had a picture of himself lying in bed with a plate of fries. He also said his refrigerator was stocked with canned rosé. I messaged him and asked if he was my soulmate.

I get that I don't make the best decisions. But I'm also not looking for someone who says things like, "It's too early to drink" or "Are you eating Doritos and drinking that expensive bottle of champagne I was saving?" That guy will beat me down. He's the same guy who goes to a bottomless mimosa brunch and fucking doesn't finish his first glass of champagne.

It's acceptable to drink on Sunday if it's at a shabby chic place that serves endless amounts of champagne. My friend Mike and I were planning a Sunday brunch.

He said, "Afterward, let's go—"

"Whoa!" I cut him off. "There is no 'afterward' with brunch. There's just napping."

"I was just thinking we could squeeze in a hike."

I shook my head at him. "I'm hiking to bed after loads of bacon."

Anyway, Canned Rosé Guy and I strangely might have a future, since most of his profile pictures are of him drinking fruity cocktails.

Back to talking about morons. To the guys who have profile pictures of themselves lying half-naked in bed, from a distance, I know your ex-girlfriend took that picture. Actually, I can totally see her underwear on the ground. I picture her wearing your shirt. She obviously snapped that picture of you before she realized what a complete douche you are.

I don't even like that term: 'douche.' When did a piece-of-shit man start getting called after something women use to clean their private parts? Why can't they be called something that relates to men? And why is it that people refer to gaining courage as "growing a pair"? Or why is it if you're brave, you have balls? Why can't it be breasts? Why don't you grow a pair of breasts? And don't even get me started on the word 'hysterical.' Please stop using that word to describe someone who is overly excited. Hysteria means uterus in Greek. Go look it up. So when you say, "Stop being hysterical," you're actually saying, "Stop being a woman." Female hysteria was once a medical disorder.

Okay, I feel better now that I've educated some people. Oh, and real quick, please stop calling wimps 'pussies.' You get why after my lecture, right?

Chapter Eighteen

THIS ISN'T THE TIME FOR YOUR RELIGION

Growing up in a town of predominantly "back porch" Baptists, I absolutely appreciate the religious diversity of LA. My mother used to say the only thing that outnumbered the churches in our town were liquor stores.

"If they build one, they've got to build the other," she'd say. "That way, they can go to church all day, and then have a short commute to the bar."

Don't think for a moment that I'm criticizing Christians. I'm not. As an agnostic who was raised in one of the most controversial religions, I've got no room to talk. For all the strange things the Baptists do, they got nothing on me.

"If anyone asks what religion you are," my mother began one day, "you tell them you're a Methodist."

"But we're—"

"Shhh," she commanded. "No one needs to know what we *really* are."

Being a Methodist in my small East Texas town did

make me pretty different. When I moved to the West Coast, though, I met all sorts of people who were much more diverse than being a different sect of Christianity.

When I met my first Jewish person, I did what I normally do with Jews and said something highly offensive; it's a gift.

"Are you named after the Fleetwood Mac song, too?" I asked my friend Sarah.

She narrowed her dark eyes at me. "Uhhh...no, I'm Jewish. I was named for the matriarch of the Hebrew Bible, the wife of Abraham."

"Oh, my mom named me Sarah with an 'h,' even though in the Stevie Nicks' song, it is spelled differently," I stated.

To be honest, Sarah without an 'h' doesn't work. I hardly acknowledge those people when I meet them. The first thing I say to a fellow Sarah is, "You spell it the right way, don't you?"

Without the 'h,' it doesn't spell 'haras' ('harass') backward.

I now have many Jewish friends in LA. I revel in the fact that I get to learn from them about traditions and history that I was never exposed to growing up. And as a bonus, because we live in a predominantly Jewish area, my daughter gets the day off school for Rosh Hashanah and Yom Kippur, days we call "Beach Days."

When my friend Nancy told me that the kids don't have school during those days, I exclaimed, "Oh my gods! It's like Christmas morning!"

I grimaced, realizing that in two short sentences, I'd offended my Jewish friend. Twice.

My friend Zoe and I meet at a Jewish deli on Friday

mornings and go hiking from there. When we were first planning a place to meet, I suggested it, since there had been a string of strange incidents related to hikers in the area.

"Nothing bad happens at a Jewish deli, right?" I reasoned.

She agreed. "And we have the special emergency number for Jews we can call."

She was referring to a sign that was posted in the parking lot next to the deli. It read, "In case of an emergency call 1-800-555-5555."

"Why is it that you Jews can't just call 9-1-1, like the rest of us?" I asked Zoe.

She laughed. "Our emergency services are better."

"Just like your hair," I said, admiring her thick, dark hair.

In LA, there's been some controversy among various Jewish communities. My friend Nancy had to educate me on eruv, a workaround that allows Jews to take their children and possessions with them outside the house on the Sabbath and Yom Kippur. This mostly affects Orthodox communities. Boundaries are set to construct the "private domain" of the eruv, marked by various things like rivers or houses. However, fishing wire has been used in many instances, to create a boundary, and apparently without issue. But then some asshole outside the Jewish community comes along and throws a fit, stating that the fishing wire is a threat to birds of prey, and then the eruv is taken down, and the Jews can't take anything outside their house.

"What do you think of this controversy?" I asked Zoe.

She shrugged. "I don't care. But I don't want birds to die."

"Oh, so you'll operate the same no matter what?" I asked, curious.

"I'm only Orthodox when I get super lazy on a Saturday night." She giggled mischievously. "Then I tell my hubby he'd better get the light, since he's the rebel amongst us."

"You're a bad Jew."

She agreed with a nod. "I'm the worst."

In all seriousness, I rely on my Jewish and Hindu friends to educate Eleanor and me. My friend Samar had her mother in town from India, and I was fascinated by the woman, making her explain all the various gods to me.

"There's a beautiful Hindu temple in the Santa Monica mountains," she said. "I'll have to take you there."

"Oh! I love that temple!" I told her.

She gave me a surprised look. "You've been there?"

"Yes, I used to take Elle there when she was a baby," I stated. "On days when it was too hot for the park, I'd take her to play on the basement floor of the temple and let her crawl around the statue of Ganesha. The monks seemed to be okay with it since it was during off hours."

The old Indian woman laughed. "You used a Hindu temple as a play place for your baby? Now I've heard it all. Samar explained that you were different."

"I figured it was better than those disgusting play places at the mall," I said.

But in all seriousness, I was fascinated by all the gods and rituals. Hinduism, an ancient and complex religion, has always been interesting to me. I think I'm more of a Zen

Buddhist, but not the revolting type who walk labyrinths on the weekend and refuse to kill spiders.

The first time I met Samar, she told me her son was named 'Krishna.' I immediately said, "From the Bhagavad Gita!"

She later told me that she didn't think a white girl like me would pick up on the reference so quickly.

"Girl, of course, I did. And besides, you're like my sista from another motha...and father...and born on another continent. And with brown skin."

One day, I was explaining to Samar and her mother about pruning flowers. "You'll want to wear gloves because the pollen will stain your hands brown and... Wait, I guess that's not a problem for you."

"Yeah, we don't need gloves, Sa-RAH," Samar's mother said.

When she says my name, she rolls the 'r' and makes it sound like a musical note. I've started introducing myself to others saying my name with that ethnic flare: "SaRAH." It earns me confused looks from people who thought I was just some white girl. Hey, I've got a pseudo-Indian mother, and my best friend is Jewish. I also have a best friend who is an accountant, but don't judge me for that.

Although my mother was really strict about my religious upbringing, I haven't continued that with Eleanor. It's mostly out of laziness, if I'm honest. George is an atheist, which I tease him about, saying it's because he lacks any creativity.

"Don't you feel the universal spirit pulsing through you?" I'll ask him because I know it pisses him off.

"No, I feel science. If it can't be proved, it's not real."

"That's shitty. Love can't be proved, and yet we feel it...well, not for each other anymore, but you get the idea."

He fucking flipped one day when Eleanor asked me where trees came from, and I said, "God."

He whipped out a biology textbook and started reading it to her. Since then, I've sort of decided we can address religion later—like once George winds up in prison for some atheism-related felony.

However, I might have slacked with her religious education a bit too much.

The other day, we passed a large building, and Eleanor says, "What's that?"

"Oh, honey, that's a church," I replied.

"What's a church?" she asked.

Oh hell.

I've fucked up if my seven-year-old doesn't know what church is. To my credit, she knows about karma and 'ten-fold,' so I'm not a devil worshipper or anything. But other assholes have apparently been trying to educate my child about religion. She came home one day and asked, "What are we?"

"People," I answered.

She rolled her lovely blue eyes, a gesture she started doing at about age two. "No, like, what religion are we?"

"I don't have one," I said and, because I'm an asshole, I added, "I'm not religious. I'm spiritual."

"Well, what am I?" she asked.

"You're whatever you want to be," I answered.

"How do I know what that is?"

Good question. "I'll teach you, and you'll explore, and one day, you'll choose. And then you might change your mind. You have to give yourself the freedom to do that."

"What do you believe in?"

I shrugged. "I believe in it all. Hindu philosophy. Jewish ideals. Christianity. But more than anything, I believe we're all connected, and God is in everything. Well, and like your father, I like science a lot. Like Dan Brown says in his new book, 'Science and religion are saying the same thing, just in a different language.'"

My daughter is used to me using fiction to explain my point. She nodded, seeming to assimilate this knowledge.

A moment later, while Eleanor was still mulling this over, I sneezed.

"God bless you, Mommy."

I turned to her, giving her a scolding look. "Where did you pick that up?"

"People say it when you sneeze."

"Yeah, but that's because they used to think that someone's soul was escaping their body," I explained. "We know better now. If you learn anything from me on this subject, let it be to check your information. Find out whether it is true, kind, and necessary."

She nodded.

"Instead, when someone sneezes, I say 'Gesundheit,' because the Germans got it right with that one."

"Aren't I mostly German?" Eleanor asked.

I nodded. "Yeah, predominantly on your father's side."

"Then is German my religion?"

I shook my head. Damn, I had seriously neglected my daughter's religious upbringing, probably in an attempt to curb my own.

I was raised in a Christian Science home.

There. I said it.

Okay, now that you've all stopped gasping, yes, I was one of those weird kids who didn't go to the doctor; if we got sick, we prayed the flu away. And I didn't get vaccines, just like the damn hippies here on the West Coast who have pretty much brought back the whooping cough epidemic.

Don't get me wrong, sometimes vaccines seem weird to me. When the doctor gave Eleanor the chicken pox vaccine, I sort of freaked out.

"Chickenpox is a rite of passage," I told her doctor.

"But it doesn't have to be," he explained.

My brain crowded with uncertainty. I have a cute chicken pox scar above my right eyebrow... What if she didn't get her own mark? Didn't she need to?

And then I remembered when my mother told me I had chicken pox at age five. I had started crying.

"I'm going to die, aren't I?" I'd asked.

"Probably," my sister said beside me in the back seat of the station wagon. "I mean, if you get sick enough you will, because Lord knows Mom isn't taking you to the doctor."

My asshole sister ate her words years later. She'd asked me to wake her up in time to watch the movie of the week, about a woman who faked a pregnancy to get her boyfriend to stay with her. Real classy stuff. Is anyone else surprised that my lovely sister has six kids?

Anyway, I remembered shaking my sister's shoulder, but she wouldn't wake up. Sweat was rolling down her forehead, and she was seemingly in a coma. I went to fetch my mother, who decided this was the perfect time for us to sit beside my sister's bed and pray.

"This isn't the time for your religion!" I yelled, nearly in tears, thinking that my sister was going to die from some virus.

"Sarah, this is precisely the time for our religion," my mother said. "When we are fearful, that's the time to strengthen our faith."

We prayed through the night, and in the morning, my sister awoke. She wasn't the least bit grateful that I'd spent the whole night reciting scripture; she was pissed that she'd missed the movie of the week.

I'm not sure what saved my sister that night, but I also don't know what was wrong with her in the first place. That's why I tend to think that science and spirituality need to be connected in my world. If I pass one lesson on to Eleanor, it will be to surround herself with as many diverse people as she can. Value others' beliefs, and they will enrich our lives. We may not all believe in the same thing, but we are all connected by a cosmic force called love.

I may not be able to see it, but I know it exists.

Chapter Nineteen

WHY IS THE GARDNER CARRYING A PISTOL?

My friend tells me that I break up with a guy in my heart long before I break up with him for real.

"It's like you do it in your head years before," Nancy explained, "then you slowly start to push them away. By the time you've built up the actual courage to do it—"

"Eons later," I interrupted, like an asshole.

She nodded. "Yes, usually at least many months later, you've already processed the breakup, and all that's left to do is divvy up the linens and such."

I grimaced at my friend. "The guys never keep the linens. Those fuckers don't get my grandmother's doilies."

"You get the point, though, Sarah."

"I left Skyler with all the furniture and the projector television," I said smugly.

"What did he leave you with?" she asked, the bitch already knowing the answer to the fucking question.

"Ten thousand dollars in credit card debt," I stated.

I still stand by it, though... Best money I ever spent.

When Skyler and I got together, I wasn't even eighteen. Having been on his own since he was seventeen, he'd sabotaged his credit way before we were a thing. That's why when we got our first apartment together in Texas and needed to furnish it, it made perfect sense that I would be the one to get a Target, Best Buy, Capital One, and Dell credit card.

Everything was working out great until I ponied up the strength to tell him I wasn't in love with him. That only took five years. Since I can't watch grown men cry, I walked away from that relationship, leaving him the house, the furniture, and the electronics. I took the debt.

Still not a single regret.

Here's what I've learned about myself after thirty-seven years: I punish myself when relationships don't go right. Think about it; I think we all do it to some degree. When I left Skyler, I firmly believed I was in the wrong. I was the heartbreaker. I was the one who couldn't make things work. Therefore, I was the one who should pay for things.

I then moved into a mother-in-law quarters above a garage owned by a family friend named Crazy Joe. We never called Joe 'crazy' to his face. But we *always* called him 'Crazy Joe' in conversation. Crazy Joe was a paranoid hoarder. So although my mother had been nice enough to help me rent the place, and four hundred and fifty dollars was a great price for all the utility bills included, I still lived in a junkyard.

I didn't care, though, because, for the first time in my adult life, I was free. I had my own home. There is no price tag you can put on that.

Later, I would associate freedom with living in LA. It

was something that movie stars and the rich did. It was something that people who were taking a risk did. People who wanted joy over comfort. Luxury over convenience.

However, those were foreign concepts when I was growing up. So when I was in my early twenties, I was barely making it. But for those few months after escaping Skyler, I felt freedom for the first time in a long time, and it was...well, a hot, hot mess, but we will get to that later.

I might be the only person to have graduated college and never attended a single party. I kept my head buried in the books, not just to avoid the relationships I didn't know how to get out of, but also because I loved college. It was the first time I'd found a true calling. And like a genie's lamp, it promised certain treasures.

"Study hard, and you'll find success." "Get a high GPA, and you'll have freedom." "Earn a great job, and you can make your own choices."

These messages were against everything my mother believed in. None of those statements revolved around a man and the security he was meant to provide me with.

I hadn't been making my own choices for a while, although I thought I had. I was a product of my mother's parenting, still operating with the mindset that love was someone who paid the bills for you. That's not a mindset I'm proud of admitting, but it is mine. I'm an asshole who isn't afraid to admit that I was operating based on wrong beliefs from the beginning. I learned, though. And when I learned better, I did better.

When I was fifteen, my mother came home with a man who she called 'the gardener.'

"Where did you get him?" I asked as the guy shoveled dirt in the backyard.

He was considerably younger than my newly divorced mother, and he wore a mustache that made me want to puke. Worse yet, his name was Maurice.

"I didn't 'get' him anywhere," she said. "He simply came back with me to unload the landscaping supplies I bought from his uncle's nursery."

"Because that's not weird," I observed.

"Oh, Sarah, you're so uptight." My mother waved a hand at me as she craned her neck to watch Maurice bend over to spread out mulch.

'The gardener' didn't return to his uncle's store after unloading the supplies. He actually didn't leave my house for a year and a half. I didn't realize it then, but my mother —who had always picked men based on the balance in their bank account—was finally choosing someone she actually liked. A sudden inheritance had changed everything for my southern debutant mother. Still, if she were allowing her heart to choose a mate for once, I wished it could have been Tom Selleck. *His* mustache was cool. Oh, and he didn't drink a bottle of Drain-o when he was a child, unlike Maurice.

Maurice and my mother, who was obviously having a mid-life crisis, landscaped the entire fifteen acres surrounding our lake house over my junior and senior year in high school. That's when I met Skyler—during an emotionally vulnerable time in my life.

I didn't realize I was learning a silent lesson. My mother, although she didn't have chalk or a chalkboard, was teaching me lifelong lessons about love and freedom. Her definition of freedom was tied to a man. And love, to her, was growing plants bought at a nursery.

For my mother, it was more about the flowers that bloomed temporarily than the long-term plans that sprouted real potential.

"The retaining wall has officially fallen into the lake," I said to her one day, as she planted a fig tree beside the front door.

"The lady at the nursery says that fig trees are fast-growing," my mother said, ignoring me. She looked up to the sky where the Texas sun was shining down. "By the spring, this plant will shield the house from the heat, providing much-needed shade. And figs are considered a romantic fruit, isn't that something?"

"So the insurance money for the retaining wall?" I asked, never in the mood for my mother's hippie talk. Shocker, right?

"I spent it on a new car," she said, motioning to the small truck that Maurice now drove full-time.

The irony that my mother was spending all her time and money on landscaping our property while it crumbled into the lake wasn't lost on me. She was also planting a fig tree to shade the roof, which was caving in.

I had loved the lake home where I grew up, but I'd also always wanted to escape that small town, knowing it wasn't right for me.

"This place suffocates me," I remember telling Skyler. "I can't do small towns where everyone knows my business."

"Then come away to Dallas with me," he said. "There's tons of computer jobs for me and lots of colleges for you."

Dallas was where I'd grown up on the weekends, where

my grandmother lived. It was the only close place to shop with real stores. However, although Dallas seemed like the best option for me, I knew, deep in my spirit, that there was a better place that was more in line with my personality. Many years later, I'd cross over Los Angeles's county border and find that place.

In Dallas, I met rich aristocrats with conservative mind-sets. Old money was the way of life. I didn't understand old money—although, later I'd realize I'd actually come from it. Even back in my early adulthood, I didn't know I was craving the fresh excitement of a city that swept over the West Coast. LA might have old money, but I think it attracts so many because it offers the chance for riches and fame to those who have nothing. It's where new generations can make their mark; hopefully, create a legacy, as my ancestors did in the South.

"The neighbors are starting to talk," I told my mother one day as she shook her head at the fig tree.

"It's quite the marvel, isn't it?" she remarked, ignoring me, per usual.

The tree had taken off, having grown almost level with the house after only a few months.

"Mom, did you hear me?" I asked her. "Maurice carries Charles' old pistols around in a holster as he does his gardening. The neighbors don't like it, as you can probably understand."

My stepfather, Charles, was known for his guns. We were in Texas, right?

Side note: When George and I were dating, back when my mother remarried Charles, I took him around my step-father's house. He'd been in the ranch house several times, which was located in an iconic place in Dallas, not far from someone closely tied to the Kennedy conspiracies. I can say no more. Anyway, on this occasion, my stepfather (twice removed...wait, I'm not sure if that's how that works) and my mother were out of town. I thought it would be fun to surprise George.

I took him around and pointed out over three hundred guns stationed in the house, most almost in plain sight: Behind a door, under the couch, inside the pantry, in the linen closet, next to the television remote.

George was a whole lot more careful in my stepfather's house after that.

However, after my mother's first divorce from Charles, he left many of his guns behind, and Maurice seemed to think he'd inherited them.

"Let the neighbors talk," my mother said. "They're just jealous."

The neighbors had *always* talked. We were the Addams family. The people with the deteriorating retaining wall and the gardener who strolled around with a machete and a pistol. Shit didn't get much more entertaining than that in our resort community, which was used to rich weekenders from Dallas. We were the locals. The ones who did strange things like carry walking sticks back and forth from the bus stop.

Freedom for my mother has been a tricky affair. I respect her for her struggles, and that shouldn't be misconstrued in this text. We all do the best with what we've been given. I think, for her, freedom was growing plants. It was new beginnings. It was making something out of barren soil. It was starting over. Learning love's lessons from her might have screwed me up, but that's no more than what most parents unknowingly do to their children. My point is, there's no blame.

The year I was going to graduate from high school, Skyler and I loaded all my belongings into his pickup truck. I didn't *want* to move to the city with a guy I didn't love. But I couldn't stay in a town that had no economy or college...there wasn't even a fucking Starbucks. I know, right?

I was my mother's child. I did what she taught me to do. I ignored my heart over the more practical needs of my lifestyle. I'm not implying that I used Skyler; looking back, it was mutual in many ways.

The day I moved to the city, everything that I'd ever written about the world was loaded into the desk that Skyler had put into his truck. The boy understood computers better than most twice his age with a formal education, but he hadn't thought to load the desk with the drawers facing inward. I lost many of those early writings on an East Texas highway, but I digress.

We can always rewrite. We can always rebuild.

"The fig tree..." I said to my mother as I was loading up, about to leave for good.

She grimaced at the towering tree. "Yeah, not such a good idea, after all."

Turns out, she'd planted it too close to the house, and it was fucking up the foundation.

"I'm sure it will be okay," I said, not really talking about the fig tree—mostly referring to the fact that Maurice had run off with the truck and a lot of money.

He and my mother had spent a year, plunging every

single dollar of her and my inheritance into making the lake property amazing. I, as a minor, didn't have access to the inheritance yet, which I didn't even know about until that year, when my siblings had come of age. I'd get this inheritance later, once I was twenty-one. In the meantime, my mother was to serve as executor, taking out money when there was a *good* need.

Japanese maples and hundreds of bags of mulch aren't cheap. There was the *good* need. Honestly, I think my mother thought that if she made that property better, renovated it, that we'd all start over.

However, one year later and we'd lost fifteen feet of land to erosion from the lake, and the flowerbeds were overgrown with weeds. It's hard to sprout a garden when there's no one there to tend to it.

She and Maurice had spent over forty thousand dollars on the plants and dirt that would later burn to the ground. However, that's a story for another time. The moral to this story relates to freedom. To taking a path and retrying over and over again until you find the right one. Sometimes our intentions are to protect ourselves, but instead, we break the very foundation we stand on. It's then that we have to grab onto a branch and find a new home.

I've found that it's best if I make that on my own, instead of relying on a man to provide it, but that took me a long, long time to be able to do successfully. My mother did what she thought was best. And when she knew better... well, she went and remarried my stepfather, Charles.

However, I came to understand my mother's plight later. She thought that freedom was plants and a young gardener.

We all misunderstand this crazy idea of freedom because it's usually tied to things like money and power.

I don't blame her for squandering my entire inheritance on landscaping materials, because we are never lost, and never broken. It's a part of the path that led me to LA and the life I love now.

However, her financial decisions are the reason that I went to community college.

Chapter Twenty

I'M NOT YOUR GETAWAY DRIVER

Because my friends give me awful advice, I went out with the guy who has thirteen siblings, if we aren't counting the step brothers and sisters (that makes it seventeen). In all honesty, he was a super nice guy. Respectful and considerate. However, I'm a minimalist. I prefer a small nuclear family. I get claustrophobic if more than two people are in the kitchen. I can't drive a minivan—we all know I'd wreck it. I hate going to restaurants with a lot of people in my party; the waiters all hate us, it takes forever to get my wine, and splitting up the check is a pain in the ass.

However, my friend Sandra told me to give the guy a shot. My instinct told me that a gigantic family was just one of many factors that made us incompatible, but I thought she might be right. He was cute, nice, and a smart engineer. Oh, and he was an entrepreneur. I sort of own my business, although I don't think of this book thing like that... I don't even consider myself an adult yet. Soon, though, I will. As soon as I finish growing.

Anyway, this guy with the giant family informed me on our first date that he also owned a smoke shop.

"Wait. You sell pot?" I asked, wondering if I was back in college.

Little known fact: I sold pot in college to businessmen who hated their jobs in IT. The venture was a small stint and mostly just paid for my books and gas money to get to community college.

Smoke Shop blushed, taking a sip of his drink. "Well, it's just a side business that I keep because it's fairly easy to run, especially after all the law changes in California."

I remembered then that in his profile picture, there had been a smoke shop behind him. My detective skills were spot-on, but like the rules, I was ignoring them.

I'm not turning up my nose at smoking pot or vaping or any of the stuff that goes on in smoke shops. However, I'm also not so naïve as to think that a person who runs one isn't going to be taking part in those activities. I have enough trouble keeping the neighbor's damn reefer smoke out of my house; I wasn't sure I could date someone who was around it all the time.

Not only did I sell pot, but I used to smoke it. Shocking, right? A college kid got high off the stash she used to supply IT guys. Take me away already.

I also smoked cigarettes for a long, long time. My mother smoked during her pregnancy with me and while breastfeeding me, so I was sort of doomed to go down that road. Since quitting over ten years ago, though, I prefer not to be around smoke. It just doesn't work for me. And it sure as hell doesn't work for Eleanor.

Smoke Shop was a nice guy, and if that was the only

lifestyle difference, I might have been able to give him another chance. However, there were too many things that just didn't jive for me. He wasn't passionate about his job, he had a strange family dynamic, and he had a mouthful of yellow teeth. Super nice guy, but just not for me.

My instincts told me that, and I ignored them.

I then continued to throw out all my rules by dating a man who was wearing a suit in his profile pictures. I have these fucking rules for a reason. Guess what? Suits was exactly like my dad, just like I had suspected. I said I didn't want to date a man who wore a suit and was an adult like my dad. This guy turned out to be a broker. Anyone care to guess what my dad does for a living? One thousand points to those of you who guessed broker. And the guy did exactly what my dad did when I cursed at the table. He fucking flinched.

I get that cursing isn't ladylike. My mother has always told me that, as she trudged around the yard in her night-gown, holding a machete and a can of O'Doul's. However, cursing is a part of who I am. It's like my southern accent—as much as I've tried to get rid of it, the drawl in my voice ain't going anywhere.

I *can* control my cursing. Not that I do a good job when I'm with Eleanor. But she understands that mommy is just expressing herself and that she isn't to say those words herself until she's old enough to understand what they mean and know when and when not to use them.

One of my friends once told Eleanor to plug her ears so she could say a bad word.

Eleanor looked directly at her and said, "Oh, just say it.

My mommy is a writer and is always using colorful words. She says it's a part of the job."

Fuck yeah, it is. When you have a book with a curse word in the title, it's a bit hard to get away from using colorful words.

Anyway, Suits and I had a pleasant time, but you could tell he wished I weren't so eccentric. Though, if I'm honest, I wished he hadn't buttoned his shirt all the way.

Because I'm an idiot, I also dated men who shared my exes' names. Talking to a guy named George just felt wrong. It was like each time I'd say or think his name, I was jinxing our relationship. And just the connotation brought old frustrations to my mind. The guy hadn't even done anything wrong when we first started talking, and I was already irritated with him.

For that reason, when I started talking to a guy named Connor, I asked him if he went by a different name.

"No, just Connor," he said good-naturedly.

"Do you ever shorten it?" I asked, trying to figure out a way around calling him by my ex's name.

"Uhhhh...I guess you could call me 'Con,'" he said tentatively.

Yeah, this wasn't going to work. My fucking exes had ruined my potential with these guys by having names. To hell with them.

I've gone back to my rules. I'm thinking of writing them out in a giant book that I put on a stone pedestal. It will be called the "Rule Book" and list all the types of guys I can't date and outline inappropriate behaviors that will dock points.

I feel like I'm beating a dead horse with going over

dating profile no-nos, but seriously, the shit I see just doesn't cut it.

Men, I get that you think you're being cute, but so many of your profiles make me want to become a nun. Problem with that is that whole cursing business. Oh, and I'd drink all the communion wine. Then I'd be out dancing across the hills, singing the songs from the Sound of Music, waiting for my Captain to come along and scowl disapprovingly at my bad behavior.

Alas, I'm going to keep dating, but here are some more tips on the profile pictures: take the toothpick out of your mouth. Didn't your mother teach you anything? Chewing gum or chewing on a toothpick makes you look trashy. My mother said so, and it's still true.

If you are planking in an urban setting in any of your photos, it's going to be a no.

I feel like this shouldn't have to be said, but apparently, my expectations for men are a bit too high. Don't put pictures of you humping anything in your profile. That is all.

To the guys who insist on posting bathroom selfies: put the seat down on the toilet behind you. I already trained one dog, I'm not training two.

Setting is so important for your profile pictures, and it keeps getting overlooked. Think about what the setting says about you. If you're in a convenience store, that tells me you either work there or you literally go nowhere of interest. Context is key, and I'm paying attention.

For instance, to the guy who took a picture of himself in a hat store, wearing one of the hats. I know that you can't afford that hat. After taking your selfie, you put the hat back on the rack and walked out of there.

The ocean is right down the road for most of us in LA. Go to Malibu, take a photo in front of the Pacific, and post that. Then I don't have to look at the popcorn ceiling behind you and wonder if you ever dust that ceiling fan. This shit is going through my head, and points are being deducted if you aren't framed just right.

To the guy who has photos of himself surfing through a killer wave: keep doing what you're doing. Nice abs. Oh, and who took that photo? Technology blows my mind.

I need to make an apology to the guy who had a picture of himself beside Adam Levine. I'm sorry I swiped right on you. I got excited and for a moment thought that Adam was on Bumble. Please ignore my interest. And to the rest of the men out there, it's cool that you met someone famous, but unless they are related to you and I'll be meeting them too, please don't use those as your profile pictures. Be real. If I've taught you anything, it's to be real.

To the guy who posted a picture that was date stamped 2007, was it not possible for you to come up with anything more recent?

I know I've said this before, but the beard problem is mostly responsible for why I can't find a date. I disqualify at least ninety-nine percent of men based on their facial hair alone. I don't even care if you have what my friend Alissa calls a "dad bod." Please just shave or at least make that shit look manageable.

Oh, and I totally care if you have a "dad bod." Again, looking for abs. All surfers, please apply.

This is a good time to give you all some important

advice: a goatee is never, ever acceptable. Look at the word. It's called a 'goatee' because that's the facial hair that a goat has. Now, you may be into goats, but although I find them cute, I don't want to date one.

Guys, please stop cutting your exes out of your photos. I can still see her arm wrapped around you. And worse yet are the dudes who black out the face. That's just weird. I'm going to guess that your photo was taken before she broke up with you and you gained fifty pounds, and that's the reason you can't just take another photo. We're going to meet up, and I'll be disappointed because you misrepresented yourself. Then, over dinner, we'll have long bouts of silence, until the customary amount of time has passed and I can leave. Let's avoid that, please.

In the bios, I'm seeing a lot of men playing the 'two truths and a lie' game. No. Just don't. This is not the opportunity for me to figure out whether you play the piano, scuba dive or can speak French. Just tell me what your hobbies are. This really doesn't have to be this difficult.

Will you dudes please stop saying you're looking for your partner in crime in your bios? We are not Bonnie and Clyde. The worse we'll ever do is take more napkins than we need from Baja Fresh. You're looking for a partner, or at least someone who can help correct your language. You're not looking for a getaway driver—and if you are, I'm totally not qualified. Let's face it, guys, we're not planning any heist. A picnic at the beach, *maybe*, where I'll double park and probably get a ticket, but that's not a real crime, or I'd have been put in jail long ago.

I can go on and on, and I'm sure I'll have to return to this topic, adding to the Rule Book. However, let me leave off on an important one. Please, for the love of all that is holy, stop describing yourself as an old soul. Your mother can describe you that way. Your best friend. Even I can say that about you after we've dated for a while and you've bought me diamond studded earrings. However, you're not allowed to call yourself an old soul. Buddha doesn't like it.

It doesn't sound cool to sell yourself as having been on the planet since the dawning of the ages. It sounds fucking conceited. And all men, no matter what, get points for confidence mixed with modesty. Those of you with your tongue hanging out in your picture and describing yourself as a "catch" are going to get thrown back into the pond.

Chapter Twenty-One

IT'S SO TRENDY IT MAKES ME PUKE

I've decided to finally do an elective surgery. After years and years of dealing with this tiresome part of my body, I'm fixing it.

Maybe the LA mentality has finally broken my self-righteous attitude. However, I'm tired of looking in the mirror and being reminded of my imperfection.

I live in a part of LA where, too many times, I do a double take because I'm pretty certain I've passed an alien in the parking lot. I turn to look and, under closer inspection, I realize that it *is* a human. Her skin might be stretched dangerously over her cheekbones, and all wrinkles around her eyes are gone, but I know my own kind when I see them, even if she's had more work done than the Golden Gate Bridge. The woman's pouty lips grimace as my Prius nearly rams into her Tesla.

Oh good, she's still capable of expression, I think as I focus back on the road.

I think that plastic surgery and all these other various

cosmetic procedures are like getting a tattoo. I don't have any tattoos, but many of my friends who do say they're addictive. You get one little birdie on your ankle and then, all of a sudden you want a ring of them. And they'd look so much better if you put a sunrise behind them. Next thing you know, you've got an entire leg sleeve depicting a huge landscape.

I think it's important to remember that, in our warped minds, we think we can always look younger, slimmer, prettier. The honest truth is that beauty is on the inside... but the fucking harsh truth is that producers don't cast people using X-rays.

I have been tempted many times by the strange services that are in abundance in my area. Some of it sounds a bit like badass science fiction, like the Platelet Rich Plasma treatment (PRP). You had me at 'plasma'! Is a gun involved? Fuck, I want a plasma gun.

And again, I've digressed.

PRP involves taking a sample of a patient's blood. They separate out the platelets and plasma from the red blood cells. They combine platelets and plasma, creating a youth potion, and apply it using microneedling. Microneedling simulates the growth of collagen to create a younger appearance. If your mind isn't blown yet, this is all happening in a shiny doctor's office during your lunch break.

Of course, in this area of LA, people don't lunch. They juice maybe. They might stop off to get a vitamin B12 shot. But filling up on carbs at the noon hour is out of the question.

I'm pretty sure that no one in this area has had a carb in over ten years.

"You should try this new juice place," Zoe encouraged me one day. "It's really trendy."

"The idea of juicing makes me want to puke, like the movie *The Notebook*."

Zoe shook her head. "It's actually really good."

"The movie or juicing?" I asked, needing to clarify.

"Juicing. You should try it."

"I'm good. I like to chew. Maybe when I'm eighty."

Zoe laughed. "It's really yummy and a total meal replacement. For only six dollars, you get a juice packed with so many nutrients."

"That does beat the cost of nachos at Baja Fresh, but the problem is that I'll be hungry in like an hour," I stated.

"I thought you were on Keto," Zoe said, giving me a disapproving look.

"Yes, which means no fruity juices," I countered.

"Except for wine," she teased.

"Hey, I have to have something to wash down all this steak and cheese," I said. "I can't totally deprive myself."

I'd picked Keto because it was the only diet where I wouldn't want to kill myself. Yes, I had to give up potatoes and pasta, but I could eat as much steak, cheese and wine as I wanted.

"I don't think you're allowed to eat *as much* of those things as you want," Zoe corrected when I told her this.

"Yes, it's just like celery, but with the Keto diet. Just stay away from the evil carbs, and you can have as much as you want on the good list."

She gave me a skeptical expression, not at all convinced.

"Hey, this is working for me," I stated. "And as a bonus, I'm not an annoying vegan talking about my non-cheese.

Seriously, can they rename their imitation of cheese to what it really is: nut paste? Stop calling it 'cheese,' assholes. Unless you can drip that stuff on chips, it's nut paste."

"You're talking about nachos again," Zoe pointed out.

"Fuck it. I have an addiction," I scolded myself.

"Nut paste doesn't have a good ring to it," Zoe observed.

"I agree," I said.

The hot new thing is a probiotic cashew cream cheese. If you get in line, you can preorder it apparently. *I know, you need the link now!* It's plant-based and gluten-free. Just imagine enjoying this healthy cheese on a rice cracker, or as I like to say, storm shelter food.

My Pilates studio recently started offering cryotherapy, an edgy treatment in LA. Athletes report it's great for recovery, but there are many other benefits to taking a nitrogen gas bath. I fucking shiver when it gets below sixty degrees in LA. However, if I could endure three minutes at a temperature between -166 and -260 Fahrenheit, I could burn an extra eight hundred calories.

The equivalent of a small plate of nachos versus three minutes of my life? Challenge accepted.

Apparently, this technology from Japan has many benefits, like it decreases anxiety, and is effective at treating cold shoulder and other conditions of the joints. Again, I'm all for shivering so that I can add potatoes back in with my steak.

I've done stranger things than sit in a nitrogen bath since moving to LA. I once took Eleanor to a salt cave.

Before you get a picture of a strange underground place with miners, you should know I'm speaking of a man-made salt cave. This is LA; we don't do natural. These salt caves can be found in a normal office building. Inside, piles of salt cover the ground and walls, and instead of a miner's cart and pickaxe, there are comfortable chairs and relaxing music. And the point is to just sit there and breathe.

Sitting and breathing is the hardest thing in the world for me to do. There's so much else to do!

This salt business is not news to the Europeans, who have been relying on the therapy for centuries. It's only that LA has popularized it with all these pop-up salt caves. Visiting a salt bath is supposed to be good for relaxation, allergies, asthma, as well as many other conditions. Unprocessed Himalayan salt is apparently rich in many minerals, and breathing salt-infused air delivers a straight shot to the nervous system.

I'm not sure what possessed me to take Eleanor to play in a salt cave when I think back. The Hindu temple was probably closed.

Being hip in LA is a lost cause. My friends have resorted to buying me clothes, which actually works.

"Do you see how wearing tailored shirts can really work for you?" Samar asked me, having bought me a silk blouse with ruffles.

I did like the pattern and feel of the fabric. However, after I wore the blouse day after day, Eleanor called me out.

"You can't wear the same thing every day, Mommy."

"Well then, I'm going to need my friends to dress me, because I'm at a loss."

It could be worse. Jane was giving me hand-me-ups from her stepchildren, clothes that they had outgrown. But hey, I don't look a gift horse in the mouth. And we all know I'm cheap enough to take clothes that a fifteen-year-old outgrew. I'm not too good for that. And that's how I ensure I'm staying up on the latest trends.

I will take credit for the bedhead movement, though. That trend is all me. When I was seven, I woke up and thought my hair looked amazing without even having to brush it. I asked my mother if I could go to school like that, ,and since she was still half-asleep, she waved me off. It turned out that day was picture day. I'd not only not brushed my hair, but I'd dressed myself and looked like a colorblind homeless person.

However, since then, I've tried to master this beach wave business. I know girls who go to the beach, and the salty winds wave past their hair, creating the perfect look. That shit doesn't work for me. But according to my stylist, I can look like Kate Hudson if I get a few products and carefully apply them to my strands.

"So let me get this straight, I'm doing my hair to make it look like I didn't do my hair?" I asked my stylist.

"Yeah, like you just got finished surfing," she replied.

"I would never go surfing, though," I admitted. "I'm too afraid of getting hit in the face with the board."

"Not to mention the sharks," she added.

Weird fact: This year, the Pacific Ocean has been unusually warm. I've lived on the West Coast for over a decade and have never, ever been in the Pacific. That shit is like fucking cryogenics but without the calorie burn. However, this year, I went into the ocean. Of course, some strange sea life took a bite out of my toe, so it looks like it will be another decade before I grace the ocean with my presence.

A guy did ask me on a surfing date. I don't know how to tell him that I have zero interest in surfing, but have no problem watching him coast those waves topless.

If I do go on the date, I'll ironically spend an hour putting tons of product in my hair so I have beach waves. I don't want to be Kate Hudson, but I'll totally settle for being her shorter cousin, twice removed.

I'll totally be ready for this date after I have my elective surgery. The damn sand always gets in my eyes when I'm at the beach, fucking with my contacts. I've worn contacts for over twenty years, and the task of putting them in and getting them to behave has gotten fucking degrading.

"All you ever do is complain about your contacts," Eleanor observed one day.

I realized she was right. I have been putting off getting LASIK surgery for many reasons, not one of them being that I am worried about the surgery. Let's be honest, it's mostly because I'm cheap and would rather keep shelling out the hundred dollars for contacts than pony up for the several-thousand-dollar surgery.

However, I'm changing. You'll continue to witness this evolution going forward.

When I was at the surgeon's office for the consultation, the nice people kept asking me, "Do you have any concerns?", "Do you have questions?", "Are you worried about anything?"

"I really don't," I stated. "Lay me down and fix my eyes, I don't really care how."

Apparently, people don't usually just nod through a consultation when someone is talking about taking a laser to their eyes.

"I've performed this surgery thousands of times," the surgeon began giving me his spiel. "And I can safely say—"

"Sounds good. Sign me up. I can't take another day in contacts," I said, cutting him off.

"So you don't have any more questions? You want to do the surgery?" he asked behind his spectacles.

"Yeah, the surgery is fine," I stated.

I *did* have a burning question, but I was too nervous to ask. I wanted to know why it was that my LASIK surgeon was wearing glasses.

Chapter Twenty-Two

PLEASE STOP SENDING ME FLOWERS

George and I actually have a romantic story of how we got together. It will make people puke.

We met when we were teenagers at a summer camp. Unlike most kids that went to normal camps where they swam and rode horses, George and I went to debate camp. No, there was no roasting marshmallows over the fire. Instead, we were huddled in the libraries, crafting briefs to strengthen our cases on global warming or renewable technology.

Hey, you've known from the beginning I'm a nerd. This debate business should come as no surprise.

My friend Jane tells me that I date the nerdiest guys.

"And *you* only care what they look like with their shirts off," I countered.

"What else really matters?" she replied.

Brains.

I'm like a fucking zombie, craving a good brain. And is it really too much to ask for a man to be smart *and* have abs? I work out, *and* I can discuss string theory. Brains and fitness aren't mutually exclusive.

Anyway, George and I fell in lust at debate camp. Then he went back to middle America and me to the backwoods of Texas. We lost touch. Stayed apart. But apparently, he never forgot me.

When I was twenty-two years old, a full seven years later, George emailed me.

"Do you remember me? From debate camp?" he said.

After I picked myself up off the ground, I responded.

Four months later, he moved across the country for me. For us to start something real.

Talk about pressure, though. I did love George, and I think I'd have married him even if he hadn't given up his life in Chicago to be with me.

I firmly believe I rebelled against my mother's teachings and married George out of love. He wasn't uber-successful, but he was smart and funny, and that's more important to me. We always won trivia night at our friend's house, which totally pissed them off. Two debaters are destined to know all the answers when paired up. However, I fell back into old ways of thinking when things started to fall apart.

It was right after we moved to LA. I'd given up my career to care for Eleanor, and George had started a new gig that he hated. Things got hard. And years went by.

Acclimating to LA wasn't difficult, though. I'd felt like a zombie for years in Oregon, not knowing how I fit in. In LA, things were different. I made friends at the grocery store, and soon had a routine that felt right. I appreciated the oddities, like that people didn't go outside when it rained. And I loved the fact that I could rotate flip-flops and Ugg boots as my only shoes.

Best of all, no one took themselves overly seriously. When I called people assholes, everyone nodded in agreement.

"Yeah, we're real jerks here," someone would remark when I'd comment on a typical LA behavior.

In a brand new city, pulsing with energy, caring for an infant and nursing a dying marriage is when I began to write.

I firmly believe it was the energy of the city that fed my creativity. I'd written before, in Oregon and since I was a child in Texas, but I was *driven* in California. I felt this drive to complete my first novel, like I might die before its completion, leaving my story untold. And then I wrote another book, and another.

I had the child I adored. I had the budding career I'd longed for. And I had the city, raw and yearning for discovery, lying at my feet.

And then there was George...

He still loved me; he's much more loyal than I am. But I'd already broken up with him in my head.

And before you start judging me with that 'marriage is forever' bullshit, try and keep an open mind. The twenty-four-year-old Sarah who married George wasn't the same girl at thirty-five. I'd fallen for this spontaneous man who would abandon his life to start a new one across the country.

Despite the fact that my mother had taught me that men provided stability, that wasn't my experience for much of my marriage. I was always worried that George might get a wild hair and quit his job. He'd often pick up hobbies and then bore of them. Finances were tough. We fought because our interests were competing.

I'm not trashing the guy. I love him to this day. But we just weren't right for each other, and we were making each other miserable.

But I stayed...for years.

Why? Because I didn't know how I'd survive on my own. I used to know, but had apparently forgotten. I had taken care of myself before. I had been a strong career woman. And then everything changed.

I was my mother, yet again.

This is not a unique issue. I recently heard an astronomical percentage regarding how many women stay in unhealthy relationships because of the rise in housing prices. It seems so silly, and yet having a home is important. Many times, women become the caregivers and, in doing so, limit their financial freedom. It's supposed to be about equality, but money is power. I'd given up a great job, losing five years in the workplace, all the while supporting George's career. I'm not complaining. I'm talking about a real issue that real women can relate to.

I have always worked. I took off four days after having Eleanor before firing up the laptop and checking emails. However, in the outrageously expensive city of LA, my part-time gigs and YA books weren't going to pay the bills. I was going to have to do something huge if I wanted to support myself and Eleanor.

And George couldn't afford to divorce me either. We were stuck.

I'd promised myself, back when I left Skyler, that I'd

never stay if I didn't want to. I wouldn't force myself into a situation where I couldn't make my own decision for freedom.

I wished I could say that I woke up one morning and decided I was taking my happiness back. It would be nice to say I stood up for what I wanted in one deliberate act of courage. The truth is that I was scared, and George didn't want to let me go.

So I just became an asshole...well, more of an asshole. I started working all the time that I wasn't with Eleanor. I produced books like I was on meth, but the kind that doesn't rot your teeth—I like my smile. I threw everything I had into creating a business that would soon support my daughter and me. And in the meantime, I pushed George away.

I wasn't mean to him... Well, besides mentioning that he talked too loudly and his breathing sort of got on my nerves. But really, I just retreated, working furiously. Planning.

In the end, he wanted out as much as I did. I have a knack for being a bitch.

If you've read this far, you know how the story progresses. I did stand up for my and my family's happiness, because at the end of the day, it wasn't just about *my* freedom. It was about Eleanor's. It was about George's.

I moved my daughter and me into the same neighborhood we'd originally lived in when we first moved to LA. However, this time, I woke up alone... unless Elle had crawled into my bed during the night. It was the exact same floor model that we'd lived in before, but this time, I had the entire master closet to myself.

You know what else I had all to myself? The bills.

But it didn't matter, because I'd gotten out of something that didn't work, even though surviving on my own was hard. I'd taken a risk. And I'd work every hour that I didn't have Eleanor in order to make this new life work.

But thankfully, I didn't have to.

George moved into his own home, not far from mine. His is a cave with all the horrid artwork I'd never allowed him to display. Mine is airy and bright with clean lines, and it's quiet. I live inside my head a lot, so I prefer my surroundings to shut the fuck up so I can hear the voices.

I've protected this new life with a fierceness, fearing that with one slip-up of the heart, my life would be tethered to another person's again. Then we'd be sharing insurance and a Spotify account, and their preferences would be fucking up my suggestions from Netflix.

That's why when I had my first serious relationship after the divorce, I chose someone who lived on the other side of the country.

"I wished we could see each other more often," Connor said over the phone.

"Do you?" I asked, challenging him like I doubted his judgment.

"Yeah, I miss you," he'd say.

"Thank you," I'd reply, because my momma taught me right.

"You know you're the love of my life?"

"Am I?" I asked, playing the devil's advocate.

We all know that I'm bad at breakups. It should come as no surprise that when George and I divorced, I gave Eleanor the completed paperwork and asked her to do a craft project with it. Don't worry! She couldn't read then. She had no idea she was doodling on a custody agreement that involved her.

I didn't think I'd ever have a need for that four-hundred-page bundle of California bullshit. Recently, though, I went to get Eleanor's passport, and it turned out that I needed the divorce paperwork.

"Can I get your copy of the divorce?" I asked George over the phone.

"What happened to your copy?" he asked.

Damn him.

It was just like when we were married and he would always ask me a ton of questions: "What kind of meat is this in the sauce?" "Did you wash my white shirt with the colors again?" "Why is there a scratch on your car?"

There was never any meat in the sauce. For some reason, George never figured out I couldn't cook. And of course I'd washed his whites with the colors; laundry is the bane of my existence. And for fuck's sake! I scratched my car at Trader Joe's, parking too close to someone! That's why I lease. In twenty-four months, that car and all its dents aren't going to be my problem.

"I guess I lost my copy of the divorce papers," I stated, looking at the beautiful drawing Eleanor had done on the back of Section 414.

When I popped over to George's house a few minutes later to get his copy, he said, "Hold on. Let me grab it."

Then he turned around and plucked it from a stack of papers on the countertop.

"Do you keep it out for evening reading?" I asked.

He gave me one of his trademark punishing stares.

I know George has never gotten over the fact that I was a bitch to him in order to push him away so he could see that we weren't right for each other. He came from a family who didn't divorce, so although we were awful together, he wouldn't admit it. Not until I was such an asshole that he was begging for a separation.

If it wasn't so awkward, I bet my exes could commiserate on how much of a bitch I am.

When I was trying to break up with Connor, I went back into asshole mode. He was sweet, and better than that, he was a nerd. I didn't mind the fact that he lived on the other side of the country, but he did.

"What do you think about, in a few months, me looking into moving to California?" he asked over the phone.

Without missing a beat, I said, "Too bad. California is closed."

"Sarah, I'm serious," he urged. "We can't live apart forever."

"Can't we?" I asked, employing my skeptical tone once again.

The truth was, I wasn't ready for some man to move into my territory. No, we wouldn't live together, but I'd feel obliged to him for moving across the country for us. Just like with George.

I spent many a quiet night in my home, relishing the solitude. The ownership. The ability to control the environment. Yes, it's nice to share a home with someone. Buddha knows I love sharing my home with Eleanor. However, I'm not ready to tell someone who isn't a minor that I'm tired of looking at their dishes or that their video game music is distracting me from the voices in my head.

Home is where the heart is and, for a while, I needed mine to be alone.

I've since decided that dates and long conversations on the phone with prospective men are okay. But I've only gotten to that point because I know that, no matter what, my home is always mine. I can't ever lose that again, because, to me, *that's* real freedom.

However, when I was with Connor, I kept pushing him away. He knew it too. To his credit, he saw potential in the relationship.

To earn my favor, he started sending me flowers. Regularly.

I knew he wanted to move closer, but that was just too much pressure.

And the more he did nice things for me, the more I felt like he was trying to buy my affection.

My friend Sue made an acute observation one day. "He's not buying you things because you want them. He's buying them because it creates a sense of obligation to him."

Oh fuck no, I thought.

Connor wanted a long-term relationship. He spoke of me like I was his Zelda. That was wonderful, but I wasn't in that place yet. I needed time. I'm still not in that place, and it's taken me a long time to be okay with that. Truthfully, I haven't been single for more than a month since I was fifteen years old. Not since I met George at debate camp, and my heart was swept away. And then Skyler asked me to move to the city with him, and the rest of my adulthood has been spent in a series of long-term relationships.

"You're the kind of girl that does relationships," my friend Jane said.

"What's that supposed to mean?" I asked.

"Some women date, but you never do," she observed. "You go out with one guy. He locks you down, and then the next six to ten years of your life are spent folding their laundry."

Fuck, she's right.

It was that conversation that triggered me to pick up the phone and call Connor. I was going to be bold and break up with him. It had taken me five years to break up with Skyler. I spent another five years trying to sever ties with George. It's not that I didn't like Connor, it's that I didn't want another serious relationship yet. His phone went to voicemail.

I thought about leaving him a message, but what was I going to say? *"Hey, I'm an asshole. Call me back when you get a chance"*?

I ended the call and opened the front door, headed for Trader Joe's.

I stopped abruptly. Looked at my doorstep with a gaping mouth.

"No! Fuck no!" I yelled, nearly stomping my feet.

There, sitting on the doorstep, was a giant bouquet of flowers. With absolute certainty, I knew who they were from. I picked up the bouquet and carried them to my neighbor's house. She'd been sick with a cold for a week.

When she opened the door to find me holding a beautiful arrangement of flowers, she burst into tears.

"Oh, my God, Sarah," she wailed. "You didn't have to do this."

I shook my head, which was hardly visible behind the

lilies. "I didn't, Nancy. Truthfully, I'm an asshole and just need you to take these off my hands."

It might have taken me another month after that, but I finally ended things with Connor.

For the first time in all my teenage and adult life, I've been single for more than six months. It's not lonely, like I would have feared. I'm not struggling to pay the bills, like my mother always feared. I don't need the constant affection of a man, like many of my soul sisters have feared.

Yes, I'm still dating. I enjoy spending time with men. However, here's the key which has taken me over half my life to figure out: I don't need a man, but I do want one. That's a big difference.

Chapter Twenty-Three

I'LL HAVE A SALAD WITH FLAXSEEDS AND A SIDE OF FUCK MY LIFE

My friends think I'm starving to death.

Before you all assume that I'm some model in Santa Monica, depriving myself for a Prada photoshoot, think again. I don't starve myself for glamour reasons; I'm just extremely lazy when it comes to eating.

"Sarah, let me stock your refrigerator," Samar texted me one day.

She and her family had stayed at my place for an afternoon while their house was being shown. I'd offered them anything in my refrigerator, which I had soon realized wasn't much.

"You really don't have to do that, although I love your chicken curry," I responded.

"I don't mind. And you don't have any food in your refrigerator. What do you eat?" she texted.

"I have food! There are carrots and cheese sticks in my icebox!"

Side note: I thought I was being good, eating carrots all the time. Turns out, according to the keto diet, they are just sticks of sugar and carbs. Which reminds me, one time when I was poor, my boss bet me twenty dollars to down a giant pixie stick in under a minute. Best twenty dollars I've ever earned. Anyway, pixie sticks are pretty much carrots but without the beta-carotene.

"You need real food," Samar continued.

Her refrigerator, in contrast, was full of leftover meals. I'm pretty sure she always has a rack of lamb in the back, just in case.

"I eat real food when I'm with Eleanor," I explained to Samar. I couldn't have her thinking I was starving my child.

"What about you?" she asked.

I shrugged at the phone, which I realized didn't answer her question. When Eleanor was with her father and I was working, I sort of forgot to eat. I've tried doing those fancy meal kits, where a box arrives with all the ingredients and instructions on how to prepare it, but that shit just goes bad sitting in my refrigerator.

After I finish working at nine o'clock at night, the last thing I want to do is mince garlic and sauté some okra.

Another side note: Samar told me the other day she bought me some okra. When I asked her why she would do such a thing, she said, "You're from the south. Everyone in the south loves okra."

Everyone but me. What's up with that furry vegetable? I'm pretty certain it's not actually edible, but batter and fry it, and no one can tell.

Back to the meal plans. They don't work for me. At nine o'clock on a Tuesday after I've been working all day, I'd rather eat a bowl of pickles and cheese while watching Netflix. I'm only going to lose couch time if I cook one of those ready-to-prepare meals, and, let's be honest, I'm going to fuck up the recipe and be disappointed in the results, and I'll just end up eating cheese and pickles anyway.

"What are you doing tonight?" Pelé asked me one Saturday evening.

I'm not very good at lying, but my instinct was to tell her I was busy. It's not that I didn't want to hang out with my friend, I just wanted to hang out with myself and my Sims. They need me.

"Why?" I asked, drawing out the word tentatively.

"Kelly has a reservation at Bavel for four people, and one of the girls just dropped out," Pelé said. "She invited you."

I opened my refrigerator. I had forgotten to shop, which plainly meant I was out of pickles and wine. *Fuck my life,* I thought, scrambling for an answer. A lot of my friends use DoorDash, but I think that just makes them lazier than me. I can go out and get my own salad, thank you very much. That way, when the order is all fucked up and they didn't cut the corn salsa, I'm the only one to blame.

"Bavel?" I asked Pelé. "Should I know that place?"

"Sarah, it's totally trending right now," Pelé explained. "It takes months to get a reservation."

"You're making it sound like I should go," I said, my mind spinning to the next problem. "Do I have to put on pants?"

"No, you should wear a dress," Pelé stated. "Something LA trendy. This is the place to be."

"I don't even know what 'LA trendy' is," I admitted. "Does that mean I can't wear a muumuu?"

She laughed because she thought I was kidding.

Pelé is responsible for turning me onto much of the LA food scene, which can be intimidating, to say the least. She was also the person to make me try In and Out Burger for the first time. She totally jacked up the experience for me. It was my fault for telling her to get me whatever she was ordering.

"Where's the bun?" I asked, pointing to the burger wrapped in lettuce.

"I got it protein style, extra lettuce, no sauce, and no salt on the fries," she explained, having picked up our order and brought it to my house.

"What's the point, then?" I asked.

"It's healthier that way."

"Why didn't you say you were going to fuck up my dinner?"

"Sarah, In and Out Burger is a staple in California. I couldn't believe you hadn't tried it yet."

Pelé had wanted to be the one who took my In and Out virginity. I told her later that she ruined the experience for me.

"I broke my Keto diet for this, and the special sauce isn't even on the burger."

I had a dream the other day that I popped a tortilla chip into my mouth. Then I remembered I was on the keto diet and I didn't eat corn, flour or potatoes. I spat out the bits of the chewed chip onto the floor and raked my hand over my tongue like I feared that any morsel might throw me out of ketosis. *I worked too hard for that to happen,* I thought.

When I woke up, I realized that my nightmares were about eating carbs. That's pretty fucked up.

"Okay, I'll go to this Bavel place, but the waiter had better not have a handlebar mustache and tell me how to eat," I said to Pelé.

"They won't," she said. "It will be great."

My friend is a total liar.

The restaurant was in the art district downtown and had giant plants hanging from the ceiling. We sat on the patio next to a couple. She was thirty years younger than him, Asian and hot. He kept passing gas when his model girlfriend got up to powder her nose—way too many times, by the way.

"Wow, the ambiance here is enough to make me puke," I said to Pelé, holding my nose.

We ended up getting several entrees to share, which is how all the cool kids eat in LA. They hadn't been raised the way I was, where you weren't supposed to eat off other people's plates.

"What's malawach?" I asked the waiter, who was pretty much done with us from the beginning when we asked to try six different wines. When we didn't like any of them, we concocted a cocktail idea that wasn't on the menu.

Danny DeVito's character in *Get Shorty* was spot-on when he said that LA people never order from the menu. It's an art form. It gets sort of difficult at places that have big menus, but I've figured out how to do it. I usually tell them I'm gluten-free, vegan, and doing the keto diet. That always stumps them.

My friend who ran a successful café told me that a famous child actor came in one day and ordered a cucumber. They didn't have cucumbers, but were they going to tell him that? Hell nah.

The waiter cleared his throat. "Malawach is an ancient grained flatbread, with grated tomato, dill crème fraiche, and a soft-boiled egg alongside a spicy strawberry zhoug sauce."

I looked at my friends. "Can we get a waiter who speaks English?"

Because my friends have much more class than me, they ordered for us, getting a plate of roasted lamb neck shawarma and foie gras halva and other things I couldn't pronounce. After paying my end of the bill, which was a small fortune, I left the restaurant completely starving.

When Pelé and I first dined together, it was at one of those gastropubs with frilly foods, and she got the avocado toast. I don't know when this became a thing, but you can't go anywhere without being hit in the face with avocado this or that. And apparently putting the vegetable on a piece of dry toast is simply divine. If these are people's standards, there might be hope for my culinary skills after all. Although, cutting into an avocado and pitting it scares the fuck out of me. I don't want to wind up like Meryl Streep and stab myself. Otherwise, I want to end up exactly like Meryl Streep.

"Are you vegan?" I asked Pelé.

She took a bite of her toast. "I am right now."

"And later?" I asked.

She shrugged. "It depends."

"You know you're going to vegan hell, right?"

She nodded. "Probably."

"There's only veal and roasted goat in vegan hell," I stated. "Only assholes and the French eat goats."

"Isn't that repetitive? 'Assholes and the French'?"

Just as popular as avocados and restaurants that serve food I can't pronounce are the food trucks. Now, I have never eaten a fish taco out of a food truck, because I have standards. Oh, and I don't eat fish. However, because I'm an asshole, I do take fish oil so I can get all the great benefits without all the fishy tastes.

"I don't eat from food trucks, either," Zoe told me when I explained my snobbish behavior.

"Because you don't want to eat food a surfer prepared from his shag wagon?" I asked.

She shook her head. "No, fancy food truck food has ruined my daughter. Now when I make a grilled cheese at home, she always rejects it, telling me she can't eat a sandwich with only one type of cheese."

Yes, the gourmet grilled cheese trend has swept through LA, leaving hipsters everywhere talking about the nutty notes they tasted in their rye bread sandwich. Don't even get me started on mac and cheese, which usually has shavings of saffron and gold sprinkled on it. And if I come across another place that wants to toss truffle oil on my fries, I'm going to scream. I want ranch and regular ketchup with my fries—and not the organic kind, either, that doesn't have sugar.

It was Zoe who told me about Barton G's restaurant. "We have to go sometime. The food is horrible, but it's an amazing experience."

"Did you hear what you just said?" I asked.

She nodded. "Yeah, but you don't go for the taste of the food. You go for the dinnertainment."

Barton G, named for its founding chef, is a restaurant where the food is transformed to take on the appearance of something that should be in a museum. For instance, the salads are served in small wheelbarrows or with a metal octopus over it. There's a lot that comes on a plate, and most of it is not edible. It's more about the presentation than it is about the taste.

The popcorn shrimp is made to look like a fast food to-go order that fell down in the backseat of a car and then loosely thrown back together. If that sounds delicious to you, then line right up and pay twenty-seven dollars for the "experience." Yes, you can go to Popeye's Chicken and get popcorn shrimp for four dollars, but you can't Instagram that shit. Not like you can at Barton G's.

"So do you want to go to Barton G's with me?" Zoe asked.

"Maybe..." I said, meaning '*fuck no.*' She hadn't really sold me on it when she stated the food was horrible.

"What if we checked out that soft serve place that makes their ice cream out of activated charcoal?" she asked.

"You do remember that I'm on keto?" I asked. "One lick of that stuff and I might go into a sugar coma. I haven't had a carb in a fortnight."

"The charcoal is supposed to be a detoxifier and could potentially whiten your teeth," she stated, continuing to make her case since she's a jerk who doesn't respect my lifestyle choices.

I flashed her a smile. "I don't need charcoal for a white smile. I gargle with hydrogen peroxide in the morning."

"Which is completely disgusting," she stated.

One time, my dentist commented on how incredibly white my teeth were.

Apparently too loudly, I announced, "I gargle with hydrogen peroxide!"

He shushed me and leaned down low. "And it obviously works, but would you mind not sharing that?"

I realized then that he offered expensive services to whiten teeth, and I was over there giving people a solution that cost only a couple of dollars. I agreed that I wouldn't tell anyone else...and then I wrote this book and mentioned it. Oops.

In all honesty, I think that my hydrogen peroxide regimen is responsible for my good health. I mean, how better to stay healthy than to disinfect your mouth upon waking up? True, it is disgusting, and in the beginning, I couldn't handle the foaming liquid for long...but now I'm a pro with white teeth.

"Doesn't charcoal compete for absorption of other nutrients?" I asked Zoe.

She gave me a surprised look. "How do you know that?"

"I'm sort of a scientist," I stated. "Well, I write science fictions novels, which is pretty much the same thing."

"Well, you have to do *something* with me," Zoe stated. "Will you go to drag queen bingo with me at Hamburger Mary's? You can get the burger wrapped in lettuce."

I grimaced, thinking of my virgin experience with In and Out Burger. I consoled myself, thinking that no one's first experience is good. I wasn't sure if I was referring to sex or In and Out Burger, though.

"Come on, Sarah," Zoe urged. "There are so many culinary experiences to be had in LA. You've got to get out and try them."

I thought for a moment. Zoe was right; I shouldn't spend another night at home eating a salad sprinkled with flaxseeds, and a side of *fuck my life*.

"Okay, fine," I stated. "But I'm not ordering from the menu. I'm going to get un-battered, fried mozzarella sticks and cauliflower fries and Brussels spout nachos."

Zoe agreed, not deterred by my high-maintenance behavior. "Which, surprisingly, might make you the biggest diva in the place."

Chapter Twenty-Four

YOUR INSTAGRAM DOESN'T QUALIFY YOU TO DATE ME

Our parents definitely had it easier, dating before the dawning age of social media. It changes everything when we have constant access to each other's profiles and status updates. I have a girlfriend who goes off Facebook every few months, telling me she's tired of seeing her ex-boyfriends' updates.

"Block them," I told Anna. "That's what I do. It's a part of the breakup regimen."

"I do, but then their comments show up in my friend's feed, and I notice he's alongside some new honey with a brand new car in his profile picture," she said.

"And then you start stalking him because you can't resist, don't you?" I asked.

"Oh, are you going to tell me you don't stalk your exes online?" she challenged.

I can honestly say that I don't, but as we've previously discussed, it's because I'm thoroughly done with them by that point.

"I try to limit my time with my exes," I stated. "There is no way I'm going to waste my time checking up on them on social media."

"But don't you want to know what they are up to?" Anna asked.

I get that it's common nature to be curious about an ex. Are they doing better since I dumped them? Do they have a girlfriend? Did they finally shave that revolting beard?

But what if I look at their profile and realize they are ten times happier than they were with me? What if I look at it and realize they got fat? What exactly is going to make me feel better? Neither scenario feels okay, so I just try and wash my hands of the whole thing.

"My problem is that I know all too well what George is up to, since he tells me regularly," I stated. "I get enough of the guy, believe me."

When we first divorced, George offered to get Eleanor piano lessons.

Awesome! Do it, I thought.

Then he comes back and tells me he bought a piano.

"Wait! What the fuck? The piano lessons are at your house?" I asked, not having expected this misdirection.

"Well, naturally," he stated. "You don't mind bringing her over to my house each week for lessons, do you?"

I could have said 'I absolutely fucking mind,' but that would have made me an asshole mother. These lessons were about *her* development, not my own frustrations. I couldn't refuse to take her to the lessons, even if I had been duped into this whole thing. *Why can't we have lessons at a music school like normal people?* I thought about buying a piano just to shove it to him, but I hate dusting furniture.

Week after week, I brought Eleanor over to my ex-husband's house and sat there during her lessons while he eyed me from the corner. Strangely, he was always working from home on the days she had lessons.

George didn't get that he was trying to keep me close even after letting me go. He firmly believed he was only offering his daughter convenient lessons in the comfort of home. I knew better.

I didn't want to stalk my ex-husband on social media; I wanted to get as far from him as possible.

"Every time George messages you about something, you scowl," Jane said to me one day.

"Well, it's usually about something revolting, like how Eleanor mentioned she can't find the stuffed animal his girlfriend gave her," I answered. "'Sarah, where's the stuffed wolf? Did you get rid of it?'" I did my George voice, which was filled with frustrated sighs.

"You stiffen up before you even view the text message he sent," Jane observed.

"I'm just used to the drama. He likes to scold me for my bad behavior." Again, I used my George voice and said, "'Eleanor says you let her sleep in your bed. Is that because you allowed her to watch Jurassic Park? She needs to sleep on her own.'"

"Well," Jane began, "why don't you change his profile picture on your phone to something that will make you laugh? That way, when he messages you, you smile instead."

That was a brilliant idea.

The next time George messaged me, a picture of a horse's ass popped up. I laughed, immediately more relaxed than before. Then I read his message: "Are you still walking

Eleanor into school? She's in second grade and can do curb-side drop off."

I was planning on holding her hand and walking her into school until she was twenty-one. Hell, if the kid still fit in my Ergo child carrier, I'd have her strapped to my chest.

George had gone out of town for a while, meaning I didn't have him stalking me while I was at his house for Eleanor's lessons. It was nice.

Then one day, we walked up to the house, and I unlocked the door.

"Hey, ladies," a bodiless voice said.

I looked around, recognizing George's voice. He was nowhere to be found. He was *supposed* to be out of town. Immediately, I wondered if he was hiding in the bushes, upping his stalker game.

"I'm up here," George said.

I looked up to see one of those Ring video cameras, peering down at us.

"Oh," I said, putting this all together.

"I got this so that even though I'm not there, I can still sort of be there," he stated.

"How nice," I said, keeping the frustration out of my voice.

"Well, and so criminals don't steal my Amazon Prime shipments," George added.

No, I didn't give a fuck what George was doing on social media. I needed more time away from him, not more infor-mation on his life. It was bad enough that I had to sit around in his house and wonder whose scarf was hanging on the coat rack, or why he had a pink yoga mat.

When my ex-boyfriend and I broke up, I blocked him

on social media immediately. That seemed like the easy solution. I'd never really looked at his profile much, since he paid for Instagram followers.

This has become a serious epidemic with the dating world. Seriously, I don't think I have enough followers to get a real catch of a man. Maybe only enough to get like a four on a scale of one to ten. I don't want to date an ugly guy, though. And guys who are tens are only dating women with over ten thousand Instagram followers.

Instagram is even hooked into the dating app, to make stalking easier. Now, not only do I get to see a man's horrible choices for profile pictures, but I also get his Instagram account, which includes the number of followers and pictures of every meal he's eaten at some dumb gastropub.

Cool, you had buffalo cauliflower and short rib tacos like every other pretentious hipster in this city. Glad you took the time to document it.

I was at a bar the other day with Pelé. Because she can easily talk to a man, she asked one for his Instagram handle.

"What does that have to do with anything?" I asked. "He's right here in the flesh and blood. Just talk to him."

Neither of them was interested in my reasoning.

He pulled up his profile on his phone and handed it to her.

"Wow, you have less than a hundred followers," she stated, reviewing his profile.

He blushed. "Well, it's mostly just my family and friends who follow me. I'm not on there very much."

She gave him a punishing look like he'd just said he didn't vote or pay his taxes.

"How many followers should I have?" the guy asked.

Pelé pulled up her own profile on his phone and showed it to him. "That's a healthy Instagram."

His eyes widened. "Whoa, you have thirty-five thousand two hundred followers?"

She tapped the screen, making it so he was now following her. "Thirty-five thousand two hundred-and-one."

I had so much to learn from this woman. All I cared about were brains and abs, but apparently, I needed to be qualifying prospective partners based on their social media presence. No wonder I was divorced.

There are so many things an Instagram profile can say about a person. When I thought about it, I realized that my ex-boyfriend's profile was mostly pictures of himself. That should have been a red flag right there. And then there were all the click farms he used.

One day, he offered to hook me up with the service, and I shook my head. "That's okay," I stated. "I don't pay people to like me."

Unfortunately, I know for a fact that my exes don't have the same policy about not stalking me on social media.

One day, Connor called me. "Hey, I noticed in the background of your picture on Instagram that your shelf looked different."

"I dusted," I stated. "It was horrible. I think I'm just going to throw out the shelf next time to make chores easier."

"Oh, I was just wondering what happened to the knick-knacks and stuff that I got for you that you used to keep there?"

I chewed on my lip, wondering how best to respond.

"Look, I got rid of that stuff. I really needed to move on, and that seemed like the best way."

"Oh," he said, the devastation heavy in his voice.

'I hate clutter' would have been a better response, but I have no tact.

If there were no social media, this wouldn't be a problem. Back in the day when a couple broke up, people had to go to great lengths to stalk each other. They might go through each other's trashcan or hide in the car down the block from their house. Now everything was out there so that anyone could find anything about anyone.

"I don't know how to keep my ex-boyfriends from stalking me on social media without being weird," I told Zoe. "I feel like I can't post anything because I worry about hurting their feelings or their mother seeing it, or one of our mutual friends."

"Your problem is real," she said with a sigh. "Just blocking them isn't enough."

I shook my head. "We're all connected, and I don't mean in the etheric, awesome way."

"Well, what you really want is for him to leave you alone, correct?" she asked.

"Yeah, exactly," I stated.

"Okay, well, why don't you do what you used to when you wanted him to leave you alone? Give him a real-world problem, and he'll get a stomachache and be out for a week. How about that?"

I smiled at my friend. "I only wish it were that easy. That only worked when we were together."

"Yeah, I always admired the way you got guys to leave

you alone when you wanted to marathon Vampire Diaries," she stated.

I'm a problem solver, but I don't know how to deal with my exes on social media. I've just decided it's a free country and let it go. They might get their feelings hurt when they see me with someone else, but their emotions are no longer mine to manage. We aren't together, and I've moved on.

"The worst is when you date a guy from the app, and then things don't work out and you go back on there," Alissa said.

"What do you mean?" I asked. "Did you match with your ex again?"

"No, but his profile came up, and before I swiped left, I read his bio," she explained. "He had all new photos and described himself as 'a man looking for a long-term relationship.'"

I shook my head. "And that's a bad thing?"

"He broke up with me because he said he wasn't ready for a long-term relationship," she replied.

I let out a sound like I'd been burned. "Damn, that's low."

Social media is a mind-fuck when it comes to dating and relationships.

I'm not a total asshole, even if I describe myself that way. I care about George and our working relationship. I often say sharing Eleanor is like we share a car. We may not get along, but we need to coordinate on car repairs and maintenance. Many times, I worry if he's off-roading with my baby or going to bring her back with her fuel low and her tires bald.

It isn't easy sharing a child, but the alternative is totally not acceptable, and I think that for all my complaints, George and I do pretty well in getting along. I didn't want to do anything to sabotage that, so when I started writing this book, I called George up.

"Hey, I wanted to tell you something."

"You're writing a book about your dating life," he said.

"Oh, so you saw?" I asked.

"Yeah, on Instagram," he answered.

Of course, the stalker did. "Yeah, well, it's really about me and how I'm an asshole. I don't mention you much."

"Much?" he inquired.

"There's a small mention of Hooker Shoes and how I'm a ruthless bitch and divorced you," I stated.

He sighed, as he always did when I mentioned the ex-girlfriend.

"I know it's got to be weird for me to have my life, our old life, out there for others to read about, but I want you to know I'll respect anything you want to keep private."

"It's okay," he said after a long moment. "Our lives have become transparent, it seems. What's the point in hiding it?"

And right then, I realized that social media had done me a favor. It had desensitized my ex to everything. If it weren't for the things he didn't want to see already being on Instagram, he might not have been so amenable.

It's weird to date in a day and age when so many have access to our lives. However, I want to believe that it means that out there is the right guy, who portrays himself on

Instagram in a way that doesn't make me want to puke. This guy would have only a couple of pictures of himself on Instagram; mostly, his profile would be snapshots of his dog and the elderly he reads to on the weekend. He'd have zero photos of his food, but dozens of pictures of the books he's reading. And his Spotify profile would look pretty much the same as mine. I really need to be with someone who shares my obsession with mellow West Coast indie music but doesn't have a beard.

Maybe I was looking at this all wrong. Maybe having access to Instagram profiles gave me the ability to disqualify the losers and bad decision-makers faster. Like, if I would have seen my ex-boyfriend's profile in the beginning, I would have found the slew of selfies, known he was obsessed with himself, and moved on.

And then there was the surgeon on Bumble. On his Instagram, he had a ton of selfies set in the operating room. *Uhhh...is it sanitary for you to be holding your phone next to that open body?* My mother would have said to overlook that and encourage the surgeon to put a ring on this finger. However, his bad Instagram decisions told me all I needed to know. Swipe left.

Just like the guy whose Instagram was full of "throwback Thursday" pictures. Dude, no one needs to see all your baby photos. You're obviously living in the past. Thank you, Instagram, for saving me from that nostalgic freak.

I'm not giving up on this dating app, or the rat-race that is dating in LA, but I might be outsourcing.

I've found that all my married friends are absolutely obsessed with swiping through my Bumble, and I have taken to loaning out my phone to them at dinner parties. They love me. They know me. They want what's best for me. I feel like they should be able to match me with a reasonable guy.

At the last party, my friend Mike and his mother sat on the couch, swiping through my dating app, trying to match me to the perfect man. A wonderful mother and son activity.

It was a bit mortifying, but I had to let it go. This was what I had come to.

And it wasn't so bad; I'd met a lot of fun people because of the dating app. I hoped to meet a lot of even better people. Ones who were right for me. Better for me than the ones I had met, than the ones who hadn't worked out. Not that there was anything wrong with my exes, but they were that for a reason.

Why was I moving forward if I wasn't going to improve? Find the person who was more compatible with me as I aged, unlike George. Find the one who I wanted around all the time, unlike my ex-boyfriends. I needed to find the man who didn't make me want to drink.

Although the guy who said that he wanted to take me day drinking on our first date might be my soulmate. We will have to see.

"Oh, Sarah!" Mike said excitedly from the couch, his mother cuddled in close to him as he swiped through my phone. "I think I found the perfect guy for you. He's into physics, art, and books." He turned the phone around so I could see the picture of the guy, who I recognized.

It was the Italian—or as I called him, Seth Rogen. A match I'd been there and done that with. He had a new profile picture and had added to his bio: "Looking for a religious woman who doesn't mind if I fall asleep on her couch."

I'd forgotten that I told Rogen the crucifix above his bed scared me. It was mostly because I was afraid of getting impaled by it during an earthquake, but he'd taken religious offense.

I laughed. "Yeah, swipe left," I told Mike. "I know Rogen."

He and his mother gave me a confused expression.

"He's nice, but we've moved on from each other," I said.

Thanks to social media, I knew that Rogen was still out there looking for his Ms. Right. And I'd helped him to figure out what he didn't want. I'm grateful I could do that for so many men.

Chapter Twenty-Five

CAN I PAY TO DO YOUR JOB?

It is more expensive to live in LA than on Mars. Okay, I get that this is a bit of an exaggeration, but still, you get the point.

There are more expensive cities in the United States to live, but still, LA remains right at the tippy-top.

For that reason, you'd think that Los Angelians would be squirreling away their money, preparing for the next housing cost spike. However, the reality is that the hipsters spend their barista tips on things that no one should pay for, the rich housewives throw money away on fake experiences, and even I have been known to be duped into giving my hard-earned cash away for something fucking ridiculous.

The other day, I paid someone so that Eleanor could brush their sheep. Yes, it's true. Afterward, I was like, *Wait! I fucking paid so my child could be a farmhand?*

I'd taken Eleanor to this commercial "family" farm outside the city. On the weekends, the city folk line up for tractor rides and fruit picking. I've gotten conned into that fruit-picking shit way too many times.

'Great, you want me to pay you extra so that I can get eaten up by bugs and pick my own damn strawberries?! Where do I sign up?'

At this place, the farmer literally said during the tour, "Most of the good strawberries have already been picked. You can buy those at the general store as you leave. But if you want the chance to hunt around just for the experience, then exit to the left."

Every fucking moron on the truck stood up. Including me.

After picking tangerines, which I couldn't eat because they weren't allowed on the Keto diet, we went and pulled up some beets. I also wasn't going to eat the dirty beets, because I'm not allowed to eat foods that grow under the ground. However, Eleanor wanted the experience of pulling up beets, so I paid for it. I did pick my own head of lettuce, which I could eat. However, I knew that was going to go to waste too. I only eat the prewashed stuff that's already chopped up in a bag. I've found that if I have to wash my vegetables, they just sit in the refrigerator. I don't have the patience to bathe my food; I hardly wash my own hair.

It wasn't lost on me that I was paying high prices to do the chores that my ancestors used the "help" for on our southern plantations.

Because nothing is too good for my princess, I paid for her to ride the pony, buy food to feed the horses, and then brush the sheep. It was at about this point that I realized I'd shelled out forty bucks to come onto this property and do the farmers' damn work.

Fuck! These farmers are brilliant.

The only thing that made me feel better was that there were loads of dumbasses like me trudging around in goat shit in their fancy shoes, buying slop from the farm to feed to the pig.

My friend Sue, who lives on one giant farm called Wyoming, keeps threatening to send me one of her goats. It's kind of an intriguing offer because I could make a fortune with just a few of the dirty animals. Hipsters would shell out big bucks to do yoga with them. They don't even care that the goats are going to piss all over their mats; that just makes the experience more fun. And since most of the goat yoga places in Malibu offer a glass of wine, I'm going to sell the hipster a can of Rosé, but label it "Farmer's Zen Concoction."

If the yoga retreat I start in the park by my house really takes off, I'm thinking of having Eleanor set up a lemonade stand. It'll actually just be a bucket of lemons. We'll sell the dumbasses lemons, make them juice them, and then Eleanor will stir in some water and sugar, and charge them for the lemonade. We'll call it the "Lemonade Experience."

You think this won't work, but I guarantee if you call it an "experience," people from LA will pay for it.

Many of the guys I date participate in mud runs. They get a cool bandana and a feeling of pride for competing in the races, but they do it for the "experience."

My father is a marine who fought in Vietnam. He speaks of spending time in the trenches, covered in mud for days, and running through the shit trying to escape the Cong. Imagine how it sounds to him when he hears that yuppies pay to have this experience.

We obviously have way too much time on our hands.

When George used to try and waste our money on these mud runs and obstacle courses, I'd offer to do it for free.

"I'll set up some hot coals and an artic enema for you in the backyard," I told him once. "We just need to have a BBQ first. When we're all done, I'll throw the coals on the grass for you to run across, then you can sprint around in circles a dozen times. Meanwhile, I'll empty the coolers of ice water we used for the drinks into a kiddie pool, and you jump into the freezing water and swim around before doing another few laps."

"You don't get it," he said, rolling his eyes at me. "It's about the *experience*."

"I like experiences," I said. "I want to have a party and get drunk and watch you be a fool. You're the one who wants to outsource this event to some fancy mud run organization. I say we keep this in-house. Support local."

"Sarah, you're not even being reasonable," he said with a growl. "Never mind. There's no talking to you." As you can see, George is the one who totally gave up on us.

My friends are always trying to recruit me for 5k runs and whatnot.

"You should totally go with us," my friend Nancy said to me one day, after explaining a run they were doing.

"I might be busy," I said, trying to come up with plans I didn't yet have. Maybe I was volunteering at the animal shelter whatever day she said this "Run for Fun" race was happening. No one runs for fun. They do it to survive. Let's name this properly: "Run for Your Life."

"It's next Sunday, and it's only twenty-five dollars to enter the race," Nancy informed me.

Oh, good, I didn't have to lie about the plans I didn't

have. Instead, I scoffed at my friend. "I'm not paying to run. That's the worst deal ever. I'll run if *you* pay *me,* though."

She gave me a look that she must have borrowed from George and rolled her eyes. "It's about the experience. It's really fun. We dress up, and afterward, there are booths and stuff."

"Okay, again, I fear that the American education system has failed us," I said, shaking my head. "You don't dress up to run; you put on clothes you don't care about or don't mind dying in."

"Well, do you want to come and watch us run?" she asked.

"I would, but I'm volunteering at the animal shelter," I said quickly.

She gave me a confused look. "On a Sunday? They're closed."

Fuck! How does she know that?

"Hey, just because the shelter is closed doesn't mean the animals get the day off," I stated. "They're still there, and in need of a bath and love, which I give them for free."

Next to the park where I hang out with the dog gang, there's this bright blue truck. It advertises that, for only fifteen dollars, you can wash your own dog inside of it.

Well, hi-de-ho! Again, put my name down. That's a mighty good deal.

I once had a boyfriend who always wanted to take me for fondue. Don't get me wrong, I'm all about big melting vats of cheese. However, he always wanted to do the meat course, where I had to skewer my protein and put it in oil. We'd have our phones out, timing each piece to ensure it was free of salmonella, but not overcooked by the time we ate it.

"Guess where I'm taking you for your birthday?" Connor said one year while he was in town visiting.

"Please don't tell me I have to cook my own food," I whined.

His smiled dropped. "No, I'm taking you to fondue."

I shook my head at him. "Yeah, that's what I mean. I'm sort of tired of paying just to cook my own food, which we both know I do badly."

Here in LA, a ton of Korean BBQ and Asian restaurants have been popping up, where the patrons are expected to grill their own food. I feel like at this point I need to rename the book *Everyone In LA Is An Idiot*.

One of the most popular Korean places in town is considered extremely pricey. Celebs can be seen sweating over their grills, getting that campfire scent locked into their hair. I'm sorry, I have no words.

But still, one of the best stories of someone being duped comes from my friend Joy. She was telling me about how she and her husband were having problems in the bedroom.

"We're seeing a therapist," she admitted one day as we were getting pedicures.

"That's probably a good idea," I said. "What do they say?"

"Well, it's sort of a special therapist," she stated a bit hesitantly.

"Yeah, they specialize in sex," I whispered, so the nice Asian lady doing my nails couldn't hear. She could totally hear, though. Let's be honest.

"Actually, it's even more different than that," Joy stated. "This person teaches us *how* to have better sex."

"Sign me up!" I said too loudly.

Joy's face flushed pink. "Yeah, the way it works is they have sex with us in order to work us through our problems."

My jaw dropped open. "You realize that you're a damn idiot, right?"

She shook her head. "No, this is legitimate."

"You're paying someone to have sex with you," I explained. "However you color that experience, it's considered prostitution."

Chapter Twenty-Six

WE DON'T TEACH SCIENCE UNTIL THEY KNOW THEIR PAGAN HOLIDAYS

One of the best reasons to live where I do is that the schools are amazing. When trying to make a decision between the options in the area, I had to choose between a full Spanish immersion school, a hippie institution, or a regular academic one. Can you guess which one I put Eleanor into?

I'm all about my child being bilingual. But this full immersion shit was never going to fly in my household. First of all, I knew that if Eleanor was learning Spanish, then that meant I was going to have to as well. I was born in raised in Texas and took years of Spanish. Presently, I fumble to ask where the bathrooms are in Mexico. The last time I was there, I relied on my friends from Montana to negotiate the bill. That's just sad.

I blame my high school Spanish teacher for my inability to retain the language. She was a witch who used to write the tests based on the students in class. I'm fucking clever and totally figured it out. The quizzes went something like this:

Question 23: Translate the phrase below:

"Sarah speaks too much in class."

Question 57: Translate the phrase below:

"Was that Sarah at the café when school was in session?"

Question 68: Translate the phrase below:

"Sarah stole the jacket from the classroom."

Yes, that bitch is why I can't speak Spanish. I blame her. And I didn't steal Sabrina's dumb rhinestone jacket. I had my very own letter jacket from being on the debate club, thank you very much.

Anyway, I want Eleanor to speak Spanish, but there was no way I was going to take a crash course in order to ensure she was fluent one day.

And then there's the hippie school. It seems to have no "real" education until close to fifth grade. They don't want to pressure the kids and make them afraid to learn with all the demands of numbers and letters. No, we wouldn't want to force Little Billy to do anything besides play with clay. Otherwise, we might crush his creative spirit. The first few grades are just learning table etiquette. That's funny, since most of the hippies I've dined with put their elbows on the table and chewed with their mouths open.

Most of the parents at this school don't allow television or video games. All the babies the parents are toting around in the schoolyard are wearing cloth diapers and have amber-teething necklaces around their neck.

And the parents are not allowed to send any waste products to school in the kid's lunch. Yes, they might have unwrapped crackers from plastic for Little Billy's lunch, but that trash can't go into the school's garbage. See no evil, and those hippies can still get into vegan heaven—which, by the way, is the quietest place in the universe since none of them have anything to talk about. What's the use in speaking when everyone there already knows you're a vegan?

I was at the park with a bunch of kids from the hippie school, and my friend had handed her phone to a group of them.

"They like listening to rap," she explained to me when I gave her a curious look.

"That makes sense," I stated. "They are six years old and from upper-class families in the suburbs."

"Hey, help me find a Lil Wayne song?" one of the shaggy kids said, not even saying 'please.'

My friend looked at the phone and said, "It's right here." Then her face softened. "That's right, they don't teach you how to read at school."

That same kid better be glad I was taught not to hit others. He sat at the table between my friend and me, saying things that only frustratingly spoiled LA children say.

"I want to go back to your house," he said to my friend.

"We can't," Sandra explained. "I have other kids at the park who I'm watching."

"Why don't you call your husband to come and take over," he pretty much demanded.

Sandra, who has way too much patience, shook her head. "My husband works."

He scoffed. "That's weird."

"Hey, that's rude, you little jerk," I cut in, having had about enough of this white boy, wannabe rapper.

He scowled at me. "I'm expressing myself. Don't suppress me."

He had no idea how close I was to suppressing him.

Eleanor goes to the academic school because *I* teach her discipline. The ship I run is real, and she knows her place as a crewmember. I'm the fucking captain; one look from me, and the kid will march to timeout without even a question. These hippie kids don't know what timeout is because that's "abandonment punishment."

It might be. But guess what? I'm not raising a little psychopath who is going to ruin people's dining experiences in every restaurant they frequent, or be a drain on society. Or worse yet, have a fucking handlebar mustache or wear dreadlocks.

One time, Eleanor asked for something in front of one of my hippie friends from the other school.

"What do we say, Elle?" I asked.

"Please," she added.

The mother looked horrified. "Oh, no. You don't have to force pleasantries on your child for me. We don't make them be polite."

Wow, that seems to be working out well for you. Your little hellions might not be going off to save the world with their bad attitude and inability to conform to the social order, but at least he can sit at a vegan restaurant and order properly. Thank the fucking gods.

Eleanor *will* say please and thank you. She'll have manners and be pleasant to be around because, at the end of the day, I'm trying to raise someone who can contribute to society by getting along with others and making them feel good about the interactions they have with her. I didn't say she had to conform. I didn't say she had to do math when she grows up. But she better fucking know how to do it.

I was raised in an academic institution that suppressed creativity and encouraged football, and look at me: I'm a science fiction author. Don't ever tell me that teaching manners and discipline suppresses a child. If that were the case, I'd never have left the town where I was born. I'd be working at the bowling alley and shopping at the flea market every weekend.

I showed up to the park one day, which I also call my second office. I looked at Sandra and rolled my eyes. "Seriously, you brought little Satan with you again." I pointed to the rude boy with long hair who I called Little Billy.

The jerk likes to correct me every-fucking-time. "My name is Echo!" he yelled at me because he wanted to test my patience.

I usually just shook my head. The parents who named their kids Blaze, Essence, Spirit, Lyric or Moon were only asking for me to make fun of their poor decision-making. If that offends you, that's fine. I'm actually offended by your offense.

I named Eleanor something classy. An actual name and not a fucking noun or verb. And you can spell it, unlike that kid Patchouli, who goes to the hippie school.

Sidebar: I knew from the beginning that I wanted to name my child Eleanor. However, one of my grandmother's name was Eleanor. Real sweet woman, but she sort of forgot to include me in the Christmas letter a few times. Joanie and Jenny-Lynne, the cousins, got put in the thirty-five-page letter for making the honor roll. Marylou got put in there for getting a job at the frozen yogurt shop. That same year, I earned my Master of Management. Thanks, Grandma. So not that I was holding grudges, but I told my mother that I was naming my child Eleanor, but to make sure the family knew it was *her* name, and not one she was being given because of someone else. Apparently, that made me a gigantic asshole, slapping the matriarch of the family straight in the face. To be honest, I believe in giving a child their own name, not naming them after another person. I realize that makes me an asshole and I've offended a fair amount of people with that statement. We've all got our opinions. Mine just makes me a jerk. Not sorry.

I'm not sure why anyone is still surprised that I do these jerk things.

Little Billy always likes to eat all my snacks and then complain that the packaging isn't biodegradable.

"You're biodegradable," I told him once.

He didn't get the joke because, at his hippie school, they don't teach them science until eighth grade, and only after they've covered all the pagan holidays.

Sandra, who must have whiskey in her bulletproof coffee, smiled at the little jerk as he demanded more food.

"Do you want some organic popcorn or a plum?" she asked him.

Her daughter picked up one of the plums and took a bite. Sandra noticed that the produce sticker was still on it.

"Let me get that for you," she said to her daughter, taking the plum and removing the sticker. Her face went slack. "Oh no, I must have gotten the conventional ones. These aren't organic."

Her daughter spat out the fruit like she'd just been told she'd ingested poison. "Am I going to be okay? What will happen to me?"

I wanted to tell her she was going to hippie hell, but I decided not to scare the child. In hippie hell, every place is air-conditioned, and showering daily is required. Self-expression is banned as well, and the only book is on tax codes. Oh, and everything has preservatives. Everything!

Sandra smiled at her daughter, although I could see the panic below her expression. "You'll be fine," she told her.

"I don't want organic popcorn!" Little Billy yelled. "I want hummus and flaxseed chips!"

Oh man, I hoped this kid wouldn't grow up and breed. However, he'd probably end up with some woman named Paisley, and they'd birth their children in the river.

Sandra shook her head at Little Billy. "No, I don't have any of that. I have fruit though. Do you want that?"

He simply scowled at her in response.

She smiled back, undeterred. "You look nice today, Echo. Did you brush your hair for picture day? It looks nice," she asked, combing her fingers through the back of his hair.

The boy grunted, like the tribal child he was.

"Seriously, how do you put up with that little shit?" I asked when the sociopath was gone.

She shrugged. "I'm used to it by now."

I, conversely, have a low tolerance for asswipes who have an entitled attitude.

Eleanor goes to a regular school with a regular curriculum, where they are expected to add and read by the first grade. I know. I'm such an asshole mom with my high expectations.

However, I will admit that the school isn't all normal; the drop-off is full of the Who's-Who of the area. It's like a red-carpet event without the expensive evening dresses and press coverage. We all know I'm not cool enough for elementary school, or even its drop-off or pick-up. That's why I always pretend like I'm on an important call when I have to congregate with the other parents at pick up time.

Many of the first conversations with these parents start with, "Where do you live?" Then they want to know what your house model is because that will tell them what income bracket you fall into.

I don't think twice about telling people I live in the townhouses at the top of the hill. Apparently, I *need* to.

"Tony's mom says we live in apartments," Eleanor told me from the backseat.

I whipped around. "What? We don't either. There's a specific difference between apartments and townhouses, not that it should matter."

She shrugged. "She just told Tony that he probably couldn't play at my house because there wouldn't be enough room since we lived in apartments."

My fingers tightened on the steering wheel. Tony's mom is a nice person, so I'm guessing her intentions were in the right place. However, it sort of burned me up that my daughter was being disqualified from playdates because we didn't have a rolling backyard and a gardener. I've had a gardener before. They aren't all that great.

Because I'm trying to vicariously live through my daughter, I enrolled her in a fancy gymnastics school. I didn't make it into the Olympics, but she can if she sucks it up and gets her damn cartwheel right.

I had no idea what I'd bargained for when I decided to start taking her to practices. Not only does she learn to master the gymnastics basics, but I get to be locked up with a bunch of parents who don't know about "quiet" time.

All these parents have to be cooped up together for an hour in a room while we watch through the viewing window as our children tumble around. And since it's a small space, others think this is the perfect time to take a call and loudly discuss stocks or remodeling.

There is a group of nannies who meet to discuss their struggles in the corner, which is always insightful to hear. Apparently, us parents are not supposed to ask if Little Billy ate that day or how many poops he had. Fuck, for a second, I thought this was *my* kid.

I don't have a nanny, though. When I'm at the park and ask a woman which kid is hers, and she says, "Oh, I'm a nanny," I won't lie, I stop talking to her. Let's be honest, we're not going to have anything to talk about. She's doing a job, and I respect that. However, at the end of the day, the kid I'm watching, I'm fully responsible for. If Eleanor robs a bank, that shit comes back on me. With Natalie the Nanny, she doesn't have the same concerns. It's just a job.

From attending my daughter's gymnastic practices, I know about all the drama in the area. I know who is getting divorced, who is looking for work, and who is sleeping with whom. Real important stuff that seeks to melt my brain. I know who is a shitty parent, because their kid throws a fit in the tiny waiting room every week and they literally ask Bratty Billy to "please stop."

Fuck! You don't *ask* a kid to behave. You put the fear of God into them.

Then there's the mom with three children, who doesn't realize the waiting room isn't her home and disregards the rest of us while she lets Bratty Billy stomp around the place. She ignores our personal space while she talks to her child loudly in a baby voice.

Again, it's quiet time, Marsha. Shut the fuck up and put your toddler on an iPad.

Bratty Billy, her middle child, who is destined for a lifetime of therapy because of his place in the birth order, kept throwing the glue across the room and stating that it was too hard to paste.

Yep, Little Billy, that's why you're living off the family trust the rest of your life.

This mom is the one I don't get. She's got a young'un strapped to her chest and is smiling at Bratty Billy while he yells in her face. Meanwhile, the rest of us are trying to scroll through Instagram, but she doesn't give a fuck that I can't hear Taylor Swift through my headphones because her son is too loud. Half an hour later, the father arrives and walks into the room. She thrusts the baby into his arms.

"Man, he stinks," the dad says too loudly, just like Bratty Billy.

Yes, I've been smelling your youngest son's shit all this time, while your middle child screams about how hard it is to fucking use glue.

I just don't get why parents don't understand how their offspring are ruining everyone else's lives. I can say that because my kid is too afraid to say anything in public usually. I've done my job. You're welcome.

In all seriousness, Eleanor is really well behaved because I'm from the south, where we don't put up with bad behavior out of fear we're stifling self-expression. Respect and manners are the cornerstones of good parenting. And that means kiddos that when in public, don't make other people want to kill you.

I'm not the nice mom who smiles while Bratty Billy says something dumb; I grimace and make threats when Eleanor misbehaves. And we try never to be boring and paste paper together when in public, or talk loudly about how good the glue tastes. I try to keep our activities real, and also entertaining.

When Eleanor and I pass a complete stranger in public carrying something, I always whisper to her, "Ask him what's in the bag."

Because no one will get mad at a child for inquiring, they usually laugh when mine says, "Hey, Mister, what you got there?"

I've fed her a few lines I'm proud of.

When we pass a man with a beard, she says, "Hey, you're not wearing that beard, it's wearing you."

All is fair, dude, your child is somewhere annoying someone, and not with awesome lines.

When we walk through the parking lot and a car speeds

by, Eleanor stomps her feet and yells, "Hey, this isn't a race track! Slow down!"

I'm grateful that we live in an area that has beautiful parks, schools, and resources. I'm sure the children will all go on to do *things*, but I'm going to be honest. They are all assholes, even mine.

Chapter Twenty-Seven

I LIVE ON A TANGENT

"You have three phone dates?" Pelé asked with disbelief.

"Yep," I said proudly.

"When?"

"Tonight," I stated.

"Wait. With three different men?"

I nodded from my place on the reformer machine. "I've slotted them in at 8:30, 9:15 and 10."

"What if one of them runs long?" she asked as I slid the strap up my leg to finish the buns series.

"It will be like a radio show. I'll be the host, and they're the guests," I explained. "I'll just have to keep them on schedule. I'll set my Google Assistant up to remind me. I'll have her say something like, 'get off the phone, bitch, you've got another caller on the line.'"

My friend Alissa gave me my Google Assistant, not because she's a good, caring friend, but because she was tired of listening to music through a shitty speaker when she came over. The first time she had dinner at my house, I used my tiny Bluetooth speaker, which had always worked just fine for me. Alissa works for a major music company, so that shit wasn't going to cut it for her.

"My ears are bleeding," she complained, listening to my music whine through the speaker.

Since I'm pretty sure I'm tone-deaf, I didn't understand what the problem was.

The next time Alissa came over, she brought me a present. "A vendor gave me a bunch of these high-end Bluetooth speakers. It's much better than that crap you make me listen to music through." She pointed to my tiny, old speaker with a bitter look.

I would be typing this book on a typewriter if I could. I have had the same laptop for ten years. Yes, because I'm cheap, but also because I was born old. New technology is weird for me to adapt to. Even after I got a new computer, I kept it in the box and used it as an ottoman for the first six weeks. Setting the thing up and moving everything over gave me serious dread. And I usually tell myself that the inferior technology I'm using is good enough. I'm trying to get over that limiting mindset.

Thankfully, my friends are helping me.

I went to grab the speaker Alissa was offering me. She pulled it back, giving me a cautious look. "You have to get rid of the crappy speaker, though. That's the deal. I won't allow you to listen to anything through that."

Damn, she was demanding. I reasoned it was for my own good.

Alissa watches my cat, Finley, when I'm out of town. I thought that meant she'd feed and water him, scoop up his poop and play with him a little. I didn't realize that meant she'd search my house, invading my privacy.

"You didn't get rid of the speaker," she texted me one day.

"I put it in the bathroom," I replied. "It's now solely the speaker Elle uses for listening to Harry Potter while she's in the bathtub."

"I told you to get rid of it," she warned.

"And I figured that since it's such a shitty speaker, it should go next to her bath so that way if it falls into the water, there's no harm."

She seemed okay with that for the moment.

However, the next time she came over, she had another gift. The Google Assistant.

"You already gave me a speaker," I said, pointing to it in the corner. "And also, you know that I hate those damn things." I scowled at the device she was holding, which was probably recording all my words.

"That's Alexa, and she's a dumb bitch," Alissa explained. "The Google Assistant is smart."

When George and I were together, he would annoy the fuck out of me by repeating himself to the dumb device.

"Alexa, turn off the living room lights."

Five seconds later, when the lazy slut hadn't done anything, he'd say, "Alexa, turn off the living room lights."

Because he likes to waste his own time and mine, he'd say it five more times. Meanwhile, I'd just get up and turn off the living room lights.

Then when I was talking to myself or scolding the cat for trying to lick the wall, Alexa would chime in, "What is that? I didn't understand."

"I wasn't talking to you, whore," I'd say. "Go back to your brothel."

"I promise you," Alissa began, "the Google Assistant is helpful. It's plugged into the search engine, and you can ask it anything."

We fired the puppy up, and I asked it the most random question I could think of.

"Okay, Google, how tall is Gary Lightbody?"

Without missing a beat, the Google Assistant answered, giving me the exact height of the lead singer of Snow Patrol, also my future husband as soon as he changes his first name. We all know I don't date Garys. Sorry, no exceptions.

"That's pretty impressive," I told Alissa.

"And it has games that will keep Eleanor busy," she stated. "However, the same rule as before applies. You have to get rid of that shitty speaker. Move the other one to the bathroom, this will be your main one."

I agreed without hesitation because I'm a liar who has no remorse. There was no way I was putting my second best speaker in the steamy bathroom where the cat was always knocking shit down, trying to trip me to get into the shower. Seriously, that fucker watches me shower every morning. He prowls back and forth in the bathroom, waiting for me to get out of the shower so he can lick up the water in the tub. It's impossible to relax with him meowing at me and watching my every move. If I lock him out, he rams his head into the door repeatedly and scratches on the wall.

I need a restraining order from my cat. He's like a bad lover. He wakes me up in the middle of the night, pounces on me first thing in the morning, demands my attention right after work, and watches me when I want privacy. I've been doing what I do in most relationships and become super neglectful in an attempt to wean him off of me. It's not working.

Since receiving Alissa's gift, I have found that the Google Assistant is actually helpful. And one of the best perks is that it's like a babysitter for Eleanor. During "quiet time," I hand her the portable speaker, and she goes into her room and asks it questions. We may not be all highbrow with a nanny, but we make do.

Okay, I kind of got off on a tangent there, but in my defense, I live on a tangent.

I'd gone from not dating at all during the summer to having three phone dates in one night. That was progress. I was getting out there, even if I was staying in so I didn't have to wear pants.

"What are phone dates?" my friend Sue asked.

"Just a chance to get to know each other briefly before we plan to drive across LA for a date," I explained.

"Is it like an interview?" she inquired. "Can you ask them stuffy interview questions like where they see themselves in five years? Or what their ideal relationship is like? Or what's their best and worst quality?"

"I think that would come off as a little intimidating," I stated.

"Yeah, and then after they answer, be all click-clacking on a computer like you're recording what they said, just like a good human resource representative would do," she said with a laugh.

"You're a sick person and will ruin my dating life if left in charge of it."

"Yeah, I will," she agreed.

Throwing yourself onto the dating market brings the hounds back to the yard, I've noticed. Not sure if that analogy works, but I mean exes. They've all come back, bringing their gifts and such.

Connor called me an hour before my back-to-back-to-back phone dates.

"Hey," he said, an awkward quality to his voice.

"Hey," I said, programming my Google Assistant with the times for the "interviews."

"I sent you a gift," he stated.

I sighed. "No," I said before I could stop myself.

"I know how much you've been wanting some diamond stud earrings," he stated proudly.

Fuck my life. I let out a measured breath. "Connor, you realize we're not together anymore, right? That means you're not supposed to buy me gifts."

"I know, but I've been thinking about it and..."

Here we are again... I interrupted him before he could do much more thinking. "You live far away. I like my space. We were great together, but I'm just not ready for what you want," I explained.

"But I think that if we just try..."

"And you sent me a present?" I asked.

That was going too far. He was trying to buy my affection, yet again. It did feel nice to be spoiled, I'm not going to lie. It was nice that he remembered I wanted another pair of studs, although diamonds...that felt serious. I wanted them, yes, but not like this. Not right then.

Finally, I shook my head. "I can't accept your gift. I'm sorry."

"What if I gave them to you in person?" he asked.

I hopped up from my reading chair. *Oh, fuck!* I looked out the window to the front step. If he was there, I was calling the cops.

Thankfully, he wasn't.

"No, that's not a good idea either," I stated.

I couldn't believe I was turning down diamond earring from a man who was offering to travel across the country to give them to me. He had all but promised to carve out his heart and give it to me on a silver platter.

I eyed the clock. My first phone date was quickly approaching.

I reminded myself that I'd taken off the summer from dating to spend time with Eleanor. But getting back to dating was for *me*. I had hardly ever been single; it wasn't fair to Connor if I took him back, and it wasn't fair to me if I didn't get out there and meet *new* people.

LA offered a long buffet of pretentious jerks and snotty assholes as potential dates, but I had hope that out there somewhere was a man who was...well, not *nice*. I don't think I could date a nice guy. I just wanted someone who could keep up with me. Someone who didn't mind it when I cursed, and also thought my dry wit was fun and not off-putting. I wanted someone who I enjoyed hearing talk about their day without me going off onto tangents in my head.

Connor was still deeply in love with me. Just as George had been. And Skyler. Although I'd always appreciated their affection, I'd never completely understood it.

I guess after all this time, I've figured out what I've been looking for. And it's much simpler than I would have thought possible, though it's something I'm not sure I've ever had; not at the age of thirty-seven, when I know who I am and what I want.

Put simply, I want someone who I'm madly in love with. I want someone who I love as much as the men in my life have loved me.

Chapter Twenty-Eight

OH GOOD, MY CHILD IS HIGH

The secret to life is to know oneself. And cheese. Smoked gouda and sharp cheddar are the fucking cornerstones of my life.

Why do I dream about melted cheese dripping off crispy chips instead of seeking a more meaningful reason for my existence? Because life is fucking hard. We're all struggling. No one is perfect. It's the reason that we medicate and drown our fears in booze and drugs. It's the reason that the beauty care industry is a multi-billion-dollar business. It's why churches stand tall, promising to offer respite for the weary traveler through this abysmal thing we call "life." None of us has it easy, because to know who we truly are is excruciatingly difficult.

And so, I've resorted to cheese.

The Pacific Ocean lapped at my feet as I pondered this conundrum of my life. From the Malibu beach, I could see Santa Monica to the south and the Channel Islands in the distance. Well, I can on a clear day, which this happened to be. The ocean is warmer this year, meaning I can actually stand it. I'm not sure that's a good thing. I should be running from every wave, trying to keep the goosebumps from rising as each swell washed over my feet. However, this year, it's almost like a warm bath, which worries me. I'm protective of this place I call home.

There are four million lost and wandering souls in Los Angeles, each trying to understand themselves.

In my own attempts to find myself, or at least some enlightenment, I've been forcing myself out of my cozy neighborhoods and exploring LA. Yes, I find myself sometimes at the Hindu temple, but I'm not really looking for myself there. Mostly, I'm just trying to learn.

The neighborhoods of LA are diverse, and I've only scratched the surface of exploring them.

When Eleanor was a baby, I thought it would be cool to take her down to Venice, the place known for its Muscle Beach. Although I did enjoy watching the surfers and weightlifters, I didn't like the contact high my child received.

On the streets of Venice, there are smoke shops on every corner, and appropriately, they're sandwiched between a taco stall and a cinnamon roll store, or something of the like. Being new to LA, I was stunned that one could go into one of the shops and apply for a medical marijuana card and walk out with the real deal. I've heard that things have gotten even easier since the laws changed. I could ask that guy I dated, Smoke Shop, but that would involve talking to him again, which might give him the wrong idea.

I remember Eleanor's eyes staring wide open as all the strange types passed on the boardwalk, their gross odors catching in the wind. Homeless men pushed carts of empty bottles and cans. Skateboarders swiveled around the chubby tourists. And guys in tank tops walked their pit bulls.

The ladies are hot, too. All of them inherited the fashion sense that skipped me, and have a body that works those halter tops and platform shoes.

Venice is the place to go to people watch.

Down the street, Santa Monica is always bursting with tourists and locals alike, seeking the ocean breeze. What I love most about it are the street performers who play for the strolling shoppers as they meander down the Third Street Promenade.

I still haven't gotten up the nerve to go to the trapeze school located on the pier, but I'm going to. One day, I'm going to be a trapeze artist, even if the circus is a sadly dying artform.

Fun fact: one time, I ran away and joined the circus. Literally. I followed them around from city to city, staying close to the ringmaster, learning everything I could. It's an obsession of mine.

When Eleanor later told me she wanted to grow up to be in the circus, I didn't scoff at the dream, like some parents. Instead, I cheered and started making plans, figuring out which act we could do together. Some mother-daughter performance where we wore bright, sequined costumes with swooping necklines. Alas, I don't think my dream will pan out, because I would absolutely loathe living in a fifth wheel.

If one takes the road from Santa Monica a bit farther, they'll wind up in the weird world of Topanga Canyon.

My friend Zoe tells me I'm not allowed to drive through

Topanga Canyon at night. Apparently, it's a hotspot for all sorts of strange sightings, like UFOs. Most of the sightings happened between 1988 and 1992; people saw glowing, yellow objects fly between the mountains. Who knows why they don't see things as much anymore. Maybe they are done spying on us. Or maybe we shot them all down.

I don't know about recent alien sightings, but I will say that they've been doing strange construction on one of the nearby roads for ages. They are always digging for something. I'm sure it has to do with pipes, but a part of my science fiction brain firmly believes they are excavating an alien's body.

The only things I've seen while going through the canyon are cyclists who apparently have a death wish and hippies who haven't showered. Although the views are breathtaking, some of the most interesting aspects of the road from the 101 to the Pacific Coast Highway are the strange houses and artwork. There's a large treehouse made almost entirely of windows. Although that limits privacy, hippies don't really care about that. Believe me, they will bathe right out in the open on that day of the month called "Bath Day." And having views of the cascading mountains is worth it to have to wash a glass house. Just don't you throw a stone, you dirty hippie.

The Sloan Oak House is named for the giant oak tree that grows through the middle of the living room. It's a landmark in Topanga and was built in the style of Frank Lloyd Wright. The house itself is modest on the outside, but the price for the two-thousand-square-foot home was almost two million dollars when it sold.

I had a tree house once. It also had great views and a

rustic feel to it. We never outgrow the urge to be amongst the trees, I guess.

The oaks in LA are regarded like gods, making new construction a mess of red tape. I like the idea of building around the trees, rather than having our majestic oaks slaughtered for new real estate. In the town of Thousand Oaks, north of LA county, no one can cut, prune, or do any work impacting the protected oak trees or their soil without a permit.

Better tell that to Little Billy before he goes off nailing something into one of the trees to make his own fort.

Although I respect Zoe's cautions regarding the strange and unexplained phenomena that happen in the canyon, that's not why I don't drive through there at night. It's plainly because I don't want to be shot. I used to hike around the canyon, but since dead bodies have been turning up all over the Santa Monica mountains, I've stayed indoors.

Sadly, there is a gunman loose who is responsible for many mysterious deaths. This person shoots at cars driving through the canyon at night. Unfortunately, there have been several fatalities seemingly related to this gunman hiding in places in the Santa Monica mountains. After more evidence came to light, the authorities were able to string together a series of shootings that happened over the years. Strange and unexplained things are always occurring in those hills, which is why I sit my ass at home on a Saturday night.

Also, if we're honest, I can't drive down the iconic Mulholland drive without pissing off the locals. *Yes, I'm riding my brake all the way down the pass.* That's how I learned to take those curves.

When I first started driving in the city of Dallas, I suddenly found myself on a six-lane highway with everyone speeding past me. I did what most inexperienced drivers would do that in that situation, and halted. That sort of pissed everyone off, creating a clusterfuck of traffic.

Then I moved to Oregon, where the roads aren't flat, and driving through mountain passes is a common occurrence. I turned down a job once because I was afraid of the commute through the steep hills.

In my defense, I was doomed from the beginning. Not because I'm truly a bad driver, but because I had been traumatized while taking driver's education. One day, I was driving the old Driver's Ed car, a beat-up Oldsmobile, with my instructor beside me. In the back seat was my friend Josh and some girl I was pretty sure was a hussy.

I was approaching a stoplight in the left lane. Wait, let me correct myself. I was approaching *the* stop light. There was only one in town. Some dumbass woman wanted to pull out of the convenience store after buying her lottery tickets and beef jerky, and another dumbass waved her across the lanes.

Later I was retaught how to drive by my mom's friend Frank, a retired naval captain. He explained that you never trust another driver to tell you when to go. He also gave me a panic attack, teaching me how to be a defensive driver.

"That person is about to pull out in front of you!" he'd scream, even though the car was parked. "What if that person suddenly opens their car door?" Frank would yell as I drove down a crowded main street. "Always be on the lookout for the things that could happen. Constant vigilance."

And that's why I can't sleep at night.

Anyway, the dumbass woman took the advice of the other driver and pulled out, ramming straight into me as I approached the stoplight.

The instructor threw his foot down on the brake stationed on his side of the car. I did the same on my side. It did no good. The cars careened into one another, buckling the front of the old Driver's Ed car that had been around for twenty years.

After checking that we were okay, the instructor got out of the car to check on the dumbass woman. She was fine. I could see that as she threw her beef jerky into the passenger's seat.

I turned around to my friend Josh, totally livid. This was going to be all around the school, and it was going to look like *my* fault. Who wrecks the Driver's Ed car? Of course, it had to be me.

"Can you believe that dumb bitch?" I yelled to him. "What an awful person."

The hussy next to him gripped her stomach, looking uncomfortable. I was about to ask if she was all right when the woman ran up to the car, yelling.

"Oh, my God! I hit the Driver's Ed car with my son in it!"

Josh's eyes widened as he recognized his mother. Then he looked at me. "I can't believe you called my mother a bitch."

I was not sorry at all. I was mortified, though. That was certain.

Hussy held her stomach, turning pale. She gripped the seat and bent over.

"Are you okay?" I asked.

"No, I don't think so," she said. "I'm pregnant, and I don't feel so good."

Of course, she was pregnant. We were all fifteen, and that's the customary age in small towns to start a family.

"Oh, fuck," I whispered under my breath.

This couldn't get any worse. I'd crashed the Driver's Ed car with a pregnant woman in it and insulted my friend's mother. Fucking wonderful. I couldn't wait to turn sixteen and drive around that godforsaken town.

Hussy, we later learned, was fine and would go on to have a slew of children. However, I was not fine. When I was finally allowed to get out of the car, I was blinded by a flash. I thought I'd been in another car wreck. Turns out what actually happened was worse: the school newspaper, having been alerted of the incident, had shown up to document the event.

Fucking delightful.

Thankfully, because I have mad debater skills that make me excellent at negotiations, I was able to convince the reporter not to print the photo in the newspaper.

The Driver's Ed instructor passed me a few weeks later, but told my mother I wouldn't be ready to drive for a while —too shaken from the events that happened.

That was true. However, what made it worse was that the dumb bitch who hit me didn't have insurance, so the Driver's Ed car was never fixed. For two more years, I had to watch that car drive around town, all the while being reminded that I had been behind the wheel when it was wrecked.

And that's why I can't drive.

The neighborhoods of LA are as unique as their people. Everyone has their favorite. And we guard our areas like we do our oak trees. I like to think that we are also fiercely protective of each other. I may talk some shit, but everyone knows where my loyalties lie.

These assholes from Santa Barbara once scoffed at me when I said that LA was my favorite city in the world.

The guy, who wore dumb prints of anchors on his button-up shirt because that's the uniform in Santa Barbara, shook his head at me. "Why LA? It's congested and dirty. It's outrageously expensive and covered in smog."

I didn't feel like pointing out that properties in Santa Barbara were even more expensive. Or that the traffic passing through Santa Barbara on the weekends always fucks up my schedule.

I shrugged. Everyone has their own ideas about LA. Some think it's overpopulated with rich assholes and wannabes. Others think it's full of beach bums who listen to Jason Mraz with the windows down. I realize that many consider the fakest people to be residents of the City of Angels. And it's all true. There are a bazillion different types of assholes here. And there's so much more. The mysteries in the Topanga mountains mixed with the history of Hollywood is one of the many reasons I love this place. There's always something new to discover. There's always another adventure around the corner. And these stories I've told have barely scratched the surface of all that I love about LA.

"The city of LA is filled with fake wannabe assholes," the Santa Barbara guy said, to which his girlfriend agreed.

"Yeah, everyone thinks they are celebrities, and the real celebrities are the worst," she stated.

"Maybe you're right," I said, not wanting to argue with two assholes who didn't see that they were calling the kettle black. But in truth, I knew that celebrities were people too, and should be treated as such.

Hollywood and LA might be full of a lot of pretentiousness. It's been described as a "loose, sprawling mess with no grid to hold anyone responsible." The people of LA might be viewed as desperate, always seeking a better appearance, placement, and position. Does all this obsession with fame create a lot of disconnected relationships? Probably. I know it's fucking difficult to date in a place where everyone has so many options. And how are we ourselves if we're constantly obsessing over image or enthralled by the images of others? But is that to say that we shouldn't respect each other for who we are, even if who we are is a bit fake?

When we think about all the strange and ostentatious things LA people do, it's because everyone is looking to this place for the next trend. In LA, we keep having to push the line, find the next new food and fashion design. Not all of them are wins, but the West Coast is one of the epicenters for showing the world what's to come. That's part of the reason that some of the behavior of its residents comes off in a way that makes us seem like such assholes, me included.

And keep this in mind: LA people could be worse. They could be from Orange County.

ACKNOWLEDGMENTS

Thank you to all the readers out there who have supported my books. I wouldn't be here writing this book if it wasn't for you. It still shocks me that you all like to read my books. I waiting to wake up and realize this was all a dream.

When I had my first professional job, there was this older man named Bob and we got along great. Shocking right? I was twenty-two and hanging out with a sixty-year old mathematician. Anyway, Bob used to call me "Weird Girl." I want to thank Michael Anderle for thinking that my weird girl tendencies are entertaining. If it wasn't for your encouragement, I never would have written this book. Really, you've done so much to foster my career and I never, ever take it for granted.

Thank you to everyone at LMBPN for all you do to get the books to the readers. Steve, I couldn't do this without your shepherding. Thank you to the editorial team and Jen for making me sound better. Thank you to the JIT team for always swooping in at the last minute.

Thank you to Jess and Jurgen for being my first readers. Your feedback is so helpful. And more than anything, I appreciate your friendship.

Jess, thanks for letting me steal your material. You will get a penny every time someone laughs at your jokes. No, I don't know how to track that, but I'll figure it out later. Actually, you're the accountant. You do it.

Thank you to my amazing support network of friends and family. I have been blessed with so many wonderful friends who nurture me and also supply awesome fodder.

Thank you to so many out there who have been sending me tips and ideas for the book. The LMBPN Ladies group on Facebook has been amazing. I heart you all.

And lastly, thank you to my daughter. This is my thirty-eighth book and as with all of them, you have been my muse. You are my love.

BOOKS BY SARAH NOFFKE

Sarah Noffke, an Amazon Best Seller, writes YA and NA sci-fi fantasy, paranormal and urban fantasy. She is the author of the Lucidites, Reverians, Ren, Vagabond Circus, Olento Research, Soul Stone Mage, Ghost Squadron and Precious Galaxy series. Noffke holds a Masters of Management and teaches college business courses. Most of her students have no idea that she toils away her hours crafting fictional characters. Noffke's books are top rated and best-sellers on Kindle. Currently, she has thirty-three novels published. Her books are available in paperback, audio and in Spanish, Portuguese and Italian. http://www.sarahnoffke.com

Check out other work by Sarah here.

Ghost Squadron:

Formation #1:

Kill the bad guys. Save the Galaxy. All in a hard day's work.

After ten years of wandering the outer rim of the galaxy, Eddie Teach is a man without a purpose. He was one of the toughest pilots in the Federation, but now he's just a regular guy, getting into bar fights and making a difference wherever he can. It's not the same as flying a ship and saving colonies, but it'll have to do.

That is, until General Lance Reynolds tracks Eddie down and offers him a job. There are bad people out there, plotting terrible things, killing innocent people, and destroying entire colonies. **Someone has to stop them.**

Eddie, along with the genetically-enhanced combat pilot Julianna Fregin and her trusty E.I. named Pip, must recruit a diverse team of specialists, both human and alien. They'll need to master their new Q-Ship, one of the most powerful strike ships ever constructed. And finally, they'll have to stop a faceless enemy so powerful, it threatens to destroy the entire Federation.

All in a day's work, right?

Experience this exciting military sci-fi saga and the latest addition to the expanded Kurtherian Gambit Universe. If you're a fan of Mass Effect, Firefly, or Star Wars, you'll love this riveting new space opera.

NOTE: If cursing is a problem, then this might not be for you. Check out the entire series <u>here</u>.

The Precious Galaxy Series:

Corruption #1

A new evil lurks in the darkness.

After an explosion, the crew of a battlecruiser mysteriously disappears.

Bailey and Lewis, complete strangers, find themselves suddenly onboard the damaged ship. Lewis hasn't worked a case in years, not since the final one broke his spirit and his bank account. The last thing Bailey remembers is preparing to take down a fugitive on Onyx Station.

Mysteries are harder to solve when there's no evidence left behind.

Bailey and Lewis don't know how they got onboard *Ricky Bobby* or why. However, they quickly learn that whatever was responsible for the explosion and disappearance of the crew is still on the ship.

Monsters are real and what this one can do changes everything.

The new team bands together to discover what happened and how to fight the monster lurking in the bottom of the battlecruiser.

Will they find the missing crew? Or will the monster end them all?

The Soul Stone Mage Series:

House of Enchanted #1:

The Kingdom of Virgo has lived in peace for thousands of years...until now.

The humans from Terran have always been real assholes to the witches of Virgo. Now a silent war is brewing, and the timing couldn't be worse. Princess Azure will soon be crowned queen of the Kingdom of Virgo.

In the Dark Forest a powerful potion-maker has been murdered.

Charmsgood was the only wizard who could stop a deadly virus plaguing Virgo. He also knew about the devastation the people from Terran had done to the forest.

Azure must protect her people. Mend the Dark Forest. Create alliances with savage beasts. No biggie, right?

But on coronation day everything changes. Princess Azure isn't who she thought she was and that's a big freaking problem.

Welcome to The Revelations of Oriceran. Check out the entire series here.

The Lucidites Series:

Awoken, #1:

Around the world humans are hallucinating after sleepless nights.

In a sterile, underground institute the forecasters keep reporting the same events.

And in the backwoods of Texas, a sixteen-year-old girl is about to be caught up in a fierce, ethereal battle.

Meet Roya Stark. She drowns every night in her dreams, spends her hours reading classic literature to avoid her family's ridicule, and is prone to premonitions—which are becoming more frequent. And now her dreams are filled with strangers offering to reveal what she has always wanted to know: Who is she? That's the question that haunts her, and she's about to find out. But will Roya live to regret learning the truth?

Stunned, #2
Revived, #3

The Reverians Series:

Defects, #1:
In the happy, clean community of Austin Valley, every-thing appears to be perfect. Seventeen-year-old Em Fuller, however, fears something is askew. Em is one of the new generation of Dream Travelers. For some reason, the gods have not seen fit to gift all of them with their expected special abilities. Em is a Defect—one of the unfortunate Dream Travelers not gifted with a psychic power. Desperate to do whatever it takes to earn her gift, she endures painful daily injections along with commands from her overbearing, loveless father. One of the few bright spots in her life is the return of a friend she had thought dead—but with his return comes the knowledge of a shocking, unforgivable truth. The society Em thought was protecting her has actu-ally been betraying her, but she has no idea how to break away from its authority without hurting everyone she loves.

Rebels, #2
Warriors, #3

Vagabond Circus Series:

Suspended, #1:
When a stranger joins the cast of Vagabond Circus—a circus that is run by Dream Travelers and features real

magic—mysterious events start happening. The once orderly grounds of the circus become riddled with hidden threats. And the ringmaster realizes not only are his circus and its magic at risk, but also his very life.

Vagabond Circus caters to the skeptics. Without skeptics, it would close its doors. This is because Vagabond Circus runs for two reasons and only two reasons: first and foremost to provide the lost and lonely Dream Travelers a place to be illustrious. And secondly, to show the nonbelievers that there's still magic in the world. If they believe, then they care, and if they care, then they don't destroy. They stop the small abuse that day-by-day breaks down humanity's spirit. If Vagabond Circus makes one skeptic believe in magic, then they halt the cycle, just a little bit. They allow a little more love into this world. That's Dr. Dave Raydon's mission. And that's why this ringmaster recruits. That's why he directs. That's why he puts on a show that makes people question their beliefs. He wants the world to believe in magic once again.

Paralyzed, #2
Released, #3

Ren Series:

Ren: The Man Behind the Monster, #1:

Born with the power to control minds, hypnotize others, and read thoughts, Ren Lewis, is certain of one thing: God made a mistake. No one should be born with so much power. A monster awoke in him the same year he received his gifts. At ten years old. A prepubescent boy with the ability to control others might merely abuse his powers, but Ren allowed it to corrupt him. And since he can have and do anything he wants, Ren should be happy. However, his journey teaches him that harboring so much power doesn't bring happiness, it steals it. Once this realization sets in, Ren makes up his mind to do the one thing that can bring his tortured soul some peace. He must kill the monster.

Note This book is NA and has strong language, violence and sexual references.

Ren: God's Little Monster, #2
Ren: The Monster Inside the Monster, #3
Ren: The Monster's Adventure, #3.5
Ren: The Monster's Death

Olento Research Series:

Alpha Wolf, #1:
Twelve men went missing. Six months later they awake from drug-induced stupors to find themselves locked in a lab. And on the night of a new moon, eleven of those men, possessed by new—and inhuman—powers, break out of their prison and race through the streets of Los Angeles until they disappear one by one into the night. Olento Research wants its experiments back. Its CEO, Mika Lenna, will tear every city apart until he has his werewolves imprisoned once again. He didn't undertake a huge risk just to lose his would-be assassins. However, the Lucidite Institute's main mission is to save the world from injustices. Now, it's Adelaide's job to find these mutated men and protect them and society, and fast. Already around the nation, wolflike men are being spotted. Attacks on innocent

women are happening. And then, Adelaide realizes what her next step must be: She has to find the alpha wolf first. Only once she's located him can she stop whoever is behind this experiment to create wild beasts out of human beings.

CONNECT WITH SARAH NOFFKE

Connect with Sarah and sign up for her email list here:

http://www.sarahnoffke.com/connect/

You can catch her podcast, LA Chicks, here:

http://lachicks.libsyn.com/

13458379R00180

Made in the USA
San Bernardino, CA
22 December 2018